Contents

Introduction

You might be reading this book because you or someone close to you is feeling overwhelmed by stress. You are not alone – every year over 13 million working days are lost in the UK due to stress and stress-related symptoms. It also accounts for 70% of visits to doctors.

Stress is a very broad term that covers anxiety and depression, and a whole range of behavioural patterns and symptoms. It is frequently talked about and is said to affect everyone to some degree every two weeks.

Stress can ruin people's lives – it can make them ill, disrupt their relationships, make them unable to work, result in lost friendships or diminished self-esteem. It is important to understand why the pace of modern-day living affects us so much, and learn how to take measures to minimise stress, whether it comes from work or our personal lives.

People are more open than they were 50 years ago, when stress was seldom mentioned. It is now more normal to talk about how you feel, but conversely, you may also feel that there is pressure on you to be a superwoman or superman and be able to cope with what life throws at you.

By reading this book you will learn:

* How to identify stress.
* How to deal with the symptoms.
* To face up to how you may be causing yourself stress.
* Some tips for coping in a crisis.
* How to adopt a lifestyle that helps you to handle stress more effectively.
* What you can do to ensure a calm and healthy approach to life.

Stress is a natural part of life and however hard we try to avoid problems, they will still occur. People will always die, divorce, be made redundant, move home or encounter traffic jams. It is quite common to try to blot out stress with negative solutions – drinking too much, smoking, taking recreational or prescription drugs, overeating, eating junk food or becoming obsessive.

It helps to recognise how you can put pressure on yourself for a variety of reasons, and to become aware of how you or others can seem reluctant to take steps to make life easier. Often situations can be improved by being honest with yourself and discovering your own motivation. You might realise that you spend a lot of time worrying about things that may not happen, and learning to manage your own behaviour can make life easier to navigate.

This book will also give you information about:

- Seeking professional help – such as counselling.

- Healthy eating.

- Exercise.

- Relaxation techniques.

- Sleeping well.

- Complementary therapies.

It may be helpful to read the whole book when you are not feeling stressed, so that you can recognise the first warning signs. If you start to take on board suggestions that help you to cope with a stressful life, you may be more able to remember what to do when stress becomes overwhelming.

If you or someone close to you is suffering from serious stress – from terminal illness for instance – there are still aspects of this book that might help to alleviate the turmoil and difficulties you are experiencing. You may want to read the parts that are relevant to you at the time, such as chapter 3, which aims to help you when problems are at their greatest.

This book aims to help you to find out how you can adopt a more positive approach to life so that you don't worry about stressful events before they happen. When they do, you have an inner strength to enable you to deal with them better and recover quicker.

'To endure is the first thing a child ought to learn, and that which he will have most need to know.'

Jean Jacques Rousseau.

Chapter One

Defining Stress

What is stress?

There are many definitions of stress, but in itself it is not a specific emotion. You feel stressed when there is too much pressure on you, which you don't feel you can cope with. A variety of different emotions may lie behind your stress including:

- Fear.
- Anger.
- Sadness.
- Guilt.
- Anxiety.

While some stressors are common to most people, everyone copes differently and one person's stress may be another person's excitement. Imagine, for instance, speaking in public. Some people just love it, while others become highly stressed just at the thought of it.

There is a difference between pressure and stress – for instance, some people thrive on working to deadlines because it gets them fired up. There may be pressure on you to perform which stimulates you, making you more able to work, more creative, focused and alert. Even though you may thrive under pressure, you are still likely to become stressed when something traumatic happens – a car accident, the death of someone close or divorce.

When you are stressed you may have negative feelings and thoughts, feel unwell, lethargic and be unable to sleep well. You may feel as if you are completely overwhelmed and unable to cope.

Many people believe that celebrities and rich people have a perfect life, but all the problems that beset others happen to them too. Often people in the limelight can't cope with the stress of it and turn to drugs or alcohol in excess.

Despite the fact that stress cannot be avoided, it is quite normal to keep waiting for it to go away. But it's far better to accept its inevitability, develop ways of dealing with it more effectively, make yourself stronger and more able to cope.

What happens when you are stressed?

'Every single one of us, be he a ruler or warrior, be he rich, middle-class, or poor, is subject to all sorts of physical and mental suffering, especially torments of the mind.'

Dalai Lama.

When you become stressed, the body kicks into the 'fight or flight' mechanism which is its natural state for avoiding danger. This is a brilliant mechanism for survival in a dangerous situation – for instance, if someone is wielding a knife or you come face-to-face with a dangerous animal – but it's hardly appropriate for modern-day situations.

When the body gets stress signals from the brain, the adrenal glands (which sit on top of the kidneys) release several hormones into the bloodstream including:

- Cortisol, which gets the body ready for action by changing its biochemistry.

- Adrenaline and noradrenaline, which raises blood pressure, increases heart rate and makes you sweat.

What you notice is that your heart pounds, your breathing becomes faster, your muscles tense, your palms get sweaty, your face goes white and your eyes dilate. What you won't notice is that insulin is released into the bloodstream to top-up your blood sugar levels. When this happens you are ready for fight or flight, and it is a very necessary situation when faced with danger.

The body reacts before you have time to think and sometimes you find these sensations are happening before you've even realised. You may also feel sick, have diarrhoea, have a dry mouth or break out into a cold sweat, and it can take some time to recover.

Prolonged stress

The problem with prolonged or frequent stress is that the body is regularly reacting as if you are facing danger. The result is that the adrenal glands become worn out and you start to feel tired, lacking in energy, depressed and many other symptoms that are associated with stress start to take effect.

When you are stressed, the body stops repairing and healing and digestion slows down, so if this continues long term you are likely to become ill.

Health problems that may result:

- Heart disease.
- High blood pressure.
- Peptic ulcers.
- Skin rashes or eczema.
- Diabetes.
- Cancer.
- Rheumatoid arthritis.
- Depleted immune system, making you less able to fight infection.
- More colds and flu.
- Depression.
- Anxiety.
- Mental illness and nervous breakdown.

Don't despair though, because there is plenty you can do to prevent getting to this stage.

What causes stress?

Everyone is different, and there are some causes of stress that affect you that may not trouble the next person. Some people find driving stressful and others love it. Some find that change of any kind stresses them out, while others thrive on it. Everyone is individual, but most people find certain situations stressful.

Because everyone is individual there are many reasons for becoming stressed. Sometimes the cause is not obvious – you may find situations stressful for no obvious reason, but because it triggers unconscious feelings or memories in you.

Below are sources of stress that are most difficult to deal with. Check how many you have experienced in the last two years.

- Death of someone close.
- Divorce or separation.
- Redundancy or loss of job.
- Loneliness.
- Financial worries.
- Caring for an elderly or sick person (one in eight British adults).
- Conflict of any kind.
- Serious illness or injury.
- Moving home.
- Retirement.
- Criminal conviction.

Just one of these is enough to cope with within a two-year period, but if it is three or more, you have had a lot to deal with.

Sometimes, an event that people associate with joy or pleasure can be stressful, such as having a baby, getting married or entertaining. All the following can cause stress too:

- Exams – for students and parents!

- Car accident.
- Traffic jams – one of the most common.
- Starting a new job.
- Starting a relationship.
- Going on holiday.
- Christmas gatherings.
- Getting married.
- Public speaking.
- Change of any kind.
- Travelling on a plane.
- Looking after children.
- Going to the dentist.
- Having a baby.

Be kind to yourself – most people feel stressed when any of these things occur, and you need to accept that. If you feel you should be able to cope with what life throws at you, remember we're all human and life can be hard.

Is it worse these days?

Everyone talks about stress a lot these days, and certainly people seem angrier. You only have to drive a car to see what kind of road rage is out there. In a recent poll, 12% of people claimed to struggle with containing their anger.

Is it our perception that stress is much worse these days or is it because we talk about it so much?

The pace of life has definitely increased in the last 20 to 30 years and technology has a lot to do with this. Everyone expects to do so much more than their grandmothers did – Monday used to be washing day and that was what they did all day! Now you expect to do several loads while getting on with your busy life because you've got a washing machine.

'Be kind to yourself – most people feel stressed when any of these things occur, and you need to accept that. If you feel you should be able to cope with what life throws at you, remember we're all human and life can be hard.'

New ways of doing things are not necessarily better. In the past you used to visit your local bank, or ring up and speak to the manager. Try doing that now and you may spend up to half an hour waiting on the phone, listening to phone prompts, soothing music, and then you get through to the wrong department or are put through to India. This all takes up your time and is very frustrating.

Without anything serious happening all this frustration adds up to bad tempers and grumpiness.

Just imagine this scenario:

- You have a row with your partner in the morning.

- You have a hard day at work with customers, boss, or colleagues harassing you.

- You have to contact your bank about a mistake they made, and you spend half an hour just trying to get through all the prompts and listening to their soothing music before you can speak to someone.

- When you drive home you get into a traffic jam.

What happens next? Do you explode or burst into tears? With all this going on around you, how can you cope? It takes a considerable lifestyle change to keep yourself positive in the face of adversity and to feel strong enough to shrug off further problems. After all, it is how you react to stressful events that affects you most.

Statistics

13.6% of all working Britons believe that their job is very or extremely stressful.

Self-reported work-related stress, depression or anxiety account for around 13.8 million lost working days per year in Britain.

High-stress jobs include teachers, nurses, professional and managerial staff, particularly in the public sector, prison officers, police officers and armed forces personnel.

UK figures from Heath and Safety Executive (HSE), www.hse.gov.uk.

Being realistic

As people get older it becomes more obvious that life presents good and bad phases. When you're in the middle of a particularly bad phase it often seems like it is going to last forever, but it generally passes, provided you don't go down with it.

There are people whose lives are very difficult from start to finish, and this book doesn't intend to diminish the problems that they have experienced at all. For most people life consists of ups and downs and when you accept that, it enables you to see light at the end of the tunnel.

Enjoying stress

It may sound like a contradiction in terms, but some people choose stress. Think of racing drivers, hang gliders and other extreme sports people.

You might identify with the buzz of doing things at the last minute, or the pressure of deadlines which sometimes makes people more creative. Some people thrive on adrenaline as it fires them up.

The only danger with living like this is that it can become addictive. Spending your life rushing around all over the place, leaving no space or time in-between, may seem like fun when you are young. But eventually it can catch up with you and you may find yourself becoming ill or burnt out.

Summing Up

- There are some serious stress events that affect most people, but you may react very differently from the next person to a whole range of stressors.

- Life is generally full of stress-inducing triggers that are impossible to avoid, so it is helpful to learn to have coping mechanisms.

- The body goes into 'fight or flight' mode when you are under stress, and if this happens too often it wears down your adrenal glands which are pumping out hormones, and leads to mental or physical illness.

- How you react to stress determines how you feel, and it is possible to develop a more positive approach to life that sees you through the bad times.

Chapter Two

Recognising Symptoms

Stress can creep up on you. You may not realise that you have taken on too much, that you're not coping, or that the health problems you are having are being caused by stress. By the time that you do recognise it, you may have become very stressed or unwell and it takes you longer to recover.

One of the keys to coping with stress is to recognise what is happening to you. It is quite common to be unaware that you are acting strangely or out of character, and those around you experience your bad moods or unusual behaviour and feel that something is wrong. Often the person who is stressed is in denial, but those who live or work with them become upset or aggravated and relationships can suffer.

How stressed are you?

To see how stressed you are, tick all the following signs that apply to you.

Mental and emotional signs:

- Forgetfulness.

- Lack of concentration.

- Being nasty to people.

- Feeling irritable.

- Lethargic.

- Losing temper.

- Mood swings.

- Constantly complaining about having too much to do.
- Rushing.
- Being late.
- Sleep difficulties/insomnia.
- Nightmares.
- Being reclusive.
- Inability to work.
- Crying a lot.
- Going over and over the same things repeatedly.
- Confusion.
- Panicky feelings.
- Dip in performance, errors and missed deadlines.
- Uncharacteristic behaviour.
- Vagueness – as if not very bright.
- Anger and tantrums.
- Violent or antisocial behaviour.
- Emotional outbursts.
- Becoming more disorganised.
- Nervous habits (biting nails, sniffing).
- Imagining illnesses.
- Feeling ill all the time.
- Lack of libido.
- Eating on the run.
- Doing several jobs at once.
- Not taking breaks at work.
- Taking work home.

- Having no time for relaxation or exercise.

- Obsessive behaviour.

- Excessive behaviour of any kind.

Physical signs:

- Upset or churning stomach.

- Irritable bowel syndrome.

- Palpitations.

- Headaches or migraine.

- Shaking or sweating.

- Diarrhoea.

- Changes to menstrual cycle.

- Hormonal imbalance.

- Spots on skin and cold sores.

- Muscle and joint aches.

- Candida – an overgrowth of yeast in the gut (causing thrush, upset stomach or athlete's foot).

- Dizziness.

- Tiredness.

- High blood pressure.

- Ulcers.

- Muscle tension.

- Back pain.

- Allergies.

- Sexual problems.

If you notch up 10 or more from both lists you are suffering from stress. If you tick 20 or more from both lists you are reaching the point where you may need to get help. You can find out how in chapter 8.

See your doctor

Worrying about your health will make you more stressed, so you need to rule out serious illness and see your doctor to have any necessary tests.

If the doctor and you conclude that it is stress related, he/she may be able to refer you to a counsellor. The GP may offer you antidepressants if you are really struggling, but although they can help you get through a sticky patch, they do not resolve the underlying problem.

Who gets stressed?

Some people definitely get more stressed about things than others, and these are sometimes defined as Type A or Type B. Tick those that apply to you and see which one you have more ticks for.

Stress type or not?

Type A

- Always early for appointments.
- Very competitive.
- Not a good listener – always interrupts.
- Always in a hurry.
- Cannot queue or wait anywhere.
- Needs to be perfect and must finish everything.
- Works very hard at a fast pace.
- Moves around quickly.

- Does not express feelings.
- Dissatisfied with work, relationships and life.
- Takes work home in the evenings and at weekends.
- Does many things at once.

Type B

- Looks at people when they speak and really listens.
- Can leave things unfinished for a while.
- Does things methodically but not in a rush.
- Speaks slowly.
- Expresses feelings.
- Takes a lunch break and does not take work home.
- Satisfied with their lot in life.
- Not everything has to be perfect.
- Does not compete with everyone and anyone.
- Waits calmly and does not get impatient.
- Takes one thing at a time.

If you have more As than Bs then you are more likely to get stressed, but if you have more Bs you are a less easily ruffled person. But it's worth remembering that even Type B will get stressed sometimes, and if you keep telling yourself that you're not the stressy type it can put even more pressure on you. Everyone changes when under extreme stress, and you may not act as you would in normal circumstances.

The only thing about Type B that can be a problem is if you are so laid-back that you are late for appointments, never finish anything and don't do tasks well – you could end up being stressed as a result!

According to research carried out at University College, London, stressed workers are more likely to suffer from heart disease due to the biological impact on the body. As part of the Whitehall II study of more than 10,000 civil servants, it was found that the under 50s who said their work was stressful were 65% more likely to develop heart disease than those who did not feel stressed. Physical effects were worse on weekdays, and those who were stressed had less time to eat well or exercise, but there were also biochemical changes in their bodies.

Published in *The European Heart Journal* online, www.eurheartj.oxfordjournals.org.

Today's climate

It's hard in this media-dominated society not to be stressed by the news. There are news bulletins every half an hour on the radio, on the Internet and regularly on the television.

If you listen to the news items you will notice that a high percentage of stories relate to murder, rape, war or terrorism. Is it any wonder that you feel stressed? If it's getting you down, switch it off.

There are some things that are completely beyond our control which may be caused by nature or by people we don't even know. Any of the following could make your life stressful:

Climate change – hurricanes, flooding, gales and other extreme weather conditions.

Change in temperatures – hotter weather for those who are not used to it can induce illness and make people irritable and stressed. Most riots take place in the summer.

Breathing in traffic fumes – this is bad for your health and your brain. It can be tiring and debilitating and can add to your feelings of not being able to cope.

Noise – if you have noisy neighbours or live close to a busy road or railway line, the noise could start to get to you, particularly if you can't sleep well. Noise pollution on a long-term basis can be very stressful.

Crowded trains – travelling five days a week on a train in rush hour with everyone pushed up against you is tiring and not great for your health.

Busy roads – traffic is on the increase all the time and journeys to work take longer and longer, leaving you feeling tired and stressed.

No wonder so many people are opting out and going to live somewhere away from it all! But life is only doom and gloom if you focus on the negative, so your best bet is to try and see the glass as half full not half empty. In the next few chapters this book helps you do that.

Ways of coping

Some people have an amazing ability to cope with stress, seemingly unaffected, while others are falling apart. This may seem good for them, but it may in truth be storing up health issues for the future. Those complementary practitioners and doctors who believe in mind/body medicine claim that unexpressed emotions remain in the body and start to gnaw away at it, causing a variety of health problems.

Some negative ways of trying to cope:

- Drinking more alcohol.
- Drinking loads of coffee.
- Overeating.
- Not eating or becoming bulimic.
- Smoking.
- Taking recreational drugs.
- Becoming addicted to prescription drugs.
- Retreating from life.
- Watching television all the time.

'If, inside, you possess good qualities, such as compassion or spiritual forgiveness . . . then external factors will not affect the internal peace of the mind.'

Dalai Lama.

- Gambling.
- Exercising to excess.
- Compulsive shopping.

It is usually hard for other people to intervene when you are doing any of these to excess. You may think that you are enjoying yourself and wonder what right anyone else has to criticise. They may be worried because if you are overindulging it is likely that you are trying to blot out the truth about how you feel.

It may feel like you are doing what you want to do and enjoying life, but it is likely that there is a deeper problem. If you can be honest with yourself and admit if you are not happy, you are already on the way to doing something about it.

There are plenty of organisations who can help you to cope with excessive behaviour of any kind, and they are listed at the back of this book. If you don't feel that you have reached the stage where you need professional help, maybe it's time to talk to a friend or try to change your habits before they get out of control.

Helping others

You might be reading this book because you want to help someone else you care about – a friend, relative, partner, son or daughter, or work colleague. It may prove difficult trying to get them to realise how stressed they are, and this may depend on the closeness of your relationship. If it is a son or daughter, wife or husband, mother or father or sibling, you may feel that it is your place to try and persuade them that they need help.

It's quite common for anyone who is stressed or angry to be in denial, blaming others for how they feel. Trying to persuade them that their behaviour is having a negative effect on others can be a thankless task because they might feel that you are criticising them and can be angry with you.

Saying that you are worried about them may be a good starting point. Let them know that the only reason you are getting involved is because you care about them.

Maybe you can encourage them to see a trained counsellor rather than to try to take the role yourself. A counsellor is objective and not emotionally involved, so the person they are helping is less inclined to take their anger out on them, or if they do, the counsellor knows how to deal with it.

Getting help

Even though we have moved on from being a 'stiff upper lip' society, Britons still don't like to ask for help. If you are suffering from a number of the symptoms listed at the beginning of the chapter, or you are feeling very unhappy, angry or sad, you might be depressed and need help.

The government has recognised that talking therapies, such as cognitive behavioural therapy (see chapter 8) are preferable to antidepressants for mild to moderate depression. There are still not enough therapists available on the NHS though, so you may be offered antidepressants instead.

Ask your GP if there is any counselling available on the NHS, and if you cannot afford to pay you may find organisations that provide free or donation-only sessions.

Summing Up

- There are many symptoms of stress and you may have some that only apply to you and not others.

- You are probably aware of how you react under stress and may recognise the physical signs as soon as they start.

- People do react differently and some seem to cope better than others, but everyone is susceptible to stress at some time in their lives.

- Recognising that you are stressed is the first step to recovery and enables you to help yourself before it becomes overwhelming.

- You may be concerned about someone else's behaviour or believe that they are depressed.

- Seeking professional help may be necessary for you or them, either on the NHS, privately or through a charity.

Chapter Three

Coping Strategies

In a crisis

You may be stressed unexpectedly by an accident, an incident, a row, or because of what someone has said or how they have behaved. Alternatively, you may already be stressed when something happens that makes you feel you can't cope anymore.

It could be the straw that breaks the camel's back, and even though it may not be a particularly stressful event in itself, you might react very strongly.

What to do in a stressful situation:

Walk away – if possible take yourself away from the stressor. Go for a walk, go home or just go outside.

Breathe – if you are shaking and showing other physical symptoms, breathe through the nose slowly and deeply, allowing air to go into your chest, diaphragm and stomach.

Be still – where possible sit (or lie) down, close your eyes, be quiet and breathe deeply.

Water – sip water – the brain needs water to function well and so does the rest of the body. It is much better than having a caffeinated drink as caffeine makes you even more hyper.

Cup of tea – chamomile or green tea would be most relaxing, but if you are wedded to your normal tea it is more likely to comfort you.

Cry or laugh – crying releases stored-up tension and generally makes you feel better. If it's not appropriate to cry publicly, go to the loo. If you can see the funny side of it at all, try to laugh.

Talk – someone else may help you to put things in perspective and not act rashly or irrationally. Provided you choose an appropriate person (not one you always argue with) they might be able to calm you down.

Wait – don't make important decisions at this time – such as leaving your partner or your job. Calm down before you do.

Beat up cushions – if you're brimming with anger rather than throwing something, hitting someone or hurting yourself, go and beat up some cushions. Alternatively kneel down, lift your arms above your head and give your bed a good bashing – it won't mind.

Lie down – when you can, lie down and close your eyes and allow yourself some time to recover.

Self-help remedies – put a few drops of Bach Flowers Rescue Remedy or Bush Flowers Emergency Essence either on the tongue or in water to calm you down instantly. They are completely safe, homeopathically prepared essences that you can buy from health food stores, chemists and online. (See chapter 11.)

A long-term approach

Being able to cope with stress is rather like practising preventative health. If you look after yourself during the good times, you have more reserves to cope with the difficult times. If you have developed a lifestyle that incorporates helpful things to do when you are stressed, it is far better than firefighting each time another stressful event occurs.

Ten steps to de-stressing your life

See how many of the following you have already adopted:

Balance work – try to have a good work-life balance (see chapter 6) so that you are not giving all your time to your job and leaving none of yourself for the rest of your life and family. Even if you love your job, you may still be stressed if you never stop working or thinking about it.

'If you can keep your head when all about you are losing theirs and blaming it all on you . . . Yours is the Earth and everything that's in it, And – which is more – you'll be a Man, my son!'

Rudyard Kipling, *If*.

Relax – learning to relax is an art. Some people may enjoy lazing around, but if you are worrying at the same time, it isn't relaxation. There are various techniques to help you to relax or you may have your own favourites, but allowing your mind to have some peace and quiet is very important to your overall wellbeing. (See chapter 9.)

Sleep – how stressed do you feel when you've had a bad night with only two or three hours of sleep? You may feel irritable, weepy or depressed. The body needs a good seven or eight hours of sleep every night to allow it to heal and recover from life's trials and tribulations. If you regularly go without a good night's sleep it may be causing you stress. (See chapter 9.)

Try complementary therapies – there's nothing more relaxing than a back or head massage, or a reflexology session – a healing foot massage. You can find out which vitamins and minerals you need to keep you in optimum health, and discover herbal remedies and flower essences that can give you a natural lift when times are hard. Most therapists spend an hour or more talking to you, which in itself is therapeutic. (See chapter 11.)

Think positive – this isn't easy to do when you are struggling with stress, so it's when you're feeling better that you need to try to change your thinking. If you are naturally cynical and negative it might help to try counselling or another kind of support to see if you can change your approach. Just looking at things in a different way can ease a lot of the stress you encounter. (See chapter 8.)

Healthy eating – a good diet means that your body is stronger and more able to fight illness which can occur when you are stressed. If you eat a lot of junk food, drink too much alcohol and caffeine or smoke, you are more likely to suffer from mood highs and lows.

Drink plenty of water – the brain needs it as much as the body and it helps you to feel well, flush out toxins and be clear thinking. When you think coffee, think water too and have one of each or, better still, just drink the water.

Exercise – this is a great stress buster as it helps to release endorphins which are known as 'happy hormones'. It keeps you healthy, in good shape and makes you feel good about yourself. When you're suffering extreme stress it's worth trying to keep up an exercise routine – just half an hour, five times a week is enough.

'Being able to cope with stress is rather like practising preventative health. If you look after yourself during the good times, you have more reserves to cope with the difficult times. If you have developed a lifestyle that incorporates helpful things to do when you are stressed, it is far better than firefighting each time another stressful event occurs.'

Talk – try talking to a friend you trust, a close relative, or to a counsellor if you don't want to share with anyone else. It's true that a problem shared is a problem halved. Keeping everything bottled up inside makes you more prone to depression, anger and unhappiness.

Be sociable – be friendly with people – the pleasures of good friendships are nurturing and supportive and can be great fun. Sometimes it makes you see that your problems aren't as bad as you think.

How you react to stress

It is how people react to difficult events that determines how stressed they feel. Some people see being made redundant as an opportunity for them to do something different, a chance to get out of a job that wasn't going anywhere, or a new beginning. Another person may see it as failure, a reason for loss of confidence, and feel pessimistic about ever being employed again.

Ask yourself why you are feeling so stressed:

- Is it fear of failure?
- Do you feel guilty?
- Has something changed in your life?
- Are you being bullied?
- Have you experienced grief in your life, which you haven't expressed?

It is often difficult to recognise when you are in a stressful situation. By talking to others who are good listeners it might make you recognise that the situation you are in – at work, at home or elsewhere – is oppressive. People become so used to their relationships with others that they often do not recognise that they are being treated badly or even bullied.

Know yourself

Understanding your own motives is often helpful in trying to make changes and improve your life.

> 'It is often difficult to recognise when you are in a stressful situation. By talking to others who are good listeners it might make you recognise that the situation you are in – at work, at home or elsewhere – is oppressive. People become so used to their relationships with others that they often do not recognise that they are being treated badly or even bullied.'

28

Negative or positive?

Remember the last stressful event that happened to you, not a major one like someone close dying or a divorce, but one that was important at the time.

For example:

* A traffic jam.
* A lengthy phone call to a bank or similar.
* Your car, computer or the Internet breaking down.
* Losing something important.
* Being late for an appointment.

How long did it take you to get over it?

(a) 10 minutes

(b) An hour

(c) Half a day

(d) A day or more

Anything more than 10 minutes is too much. You could react differently.

See the table overleaf to find out whether your reactions are positive or negative.

What could you do in a traffic jam?

* You can't do anything about it.
* You are not in danger.
* You could relax and listen to the car radio or other music you have.
* Provided you can turn your engine off, you might be able to read or even plan some work.

However important your journey is there is nothing in the world that can change the situation so if you miss the meeting, dentist appointment, funeral or wedding, being stressed doesn't improve the situation one bit.

Is your reaction negative or positive? Tick which your reaction is:

Did you think it was a disaster?	OR	Did you think, 'we'll soon sort this out?'
Did you think, 'how will I cope?'	OR	Did you believe you would cope?
Did you get very angry?	OR	Did you try to remedy the situation?
Did you blame someone?	OR	Did you recognise that blaming was pointless?
Did you get into a bad mood?	OR	Did you talk about it and get it off your chest?
Did you throw it out the window?	OR	Did you walk away for a while?
Did you get very anxious?	OR	Did you ask for help?
Did you start to panic?	OR	Did you take a few breaths to calm down?
Did you think, 'why me again?'	OR	Did you think, 'what can I learn from this?'

Even if all of your answers are negative, the purpose of this exercise is not to give yourself a hard time. It is a tool to let you see how you could help to make your own life easier.

'Nothing is a waste of time if you use the experience wisely.'

Rodin.

Some simple solutions

Becoming more aware of why you do things and scrutinising your own behaviour often takes you halfway to improving the situation. There is plenty you can do to help yourself, but if you feel that your feelings are out of control it can be useful to seek professional help (See chapter 8).

Ask yourself:

- Do you really listen when people try to help you?
- Do you write off any advice or guidance from someone who you believe is ridiculously positive (as opposed to your reality of being negative)?

- Are statements you make really true, or are they your perception of events? (My boss thinks I'm useless, I'll be the first to be fired, my partner doesn't love me, I don't have any friends).

- Could you do something about situations before reacting negatively?

- Does anyone ever tell you that you are negative, but you are quite convinced that they are wrong?

- Is your anxiety about situations borne out of a lack of self-esteem – do you really like yourself?

- Do you automatically blame yourself for things that go wrong? Is that rational?

- Does blaming yourself make anything any better?

- Is this event so traumatic that you will never forget it?

- Are you agonising about something over which you have no control?

- Are you trying to make other people change?

- Could you look at this situation another way? From the other person's point of view?

- Do you use the word 'should' a lot? *Should* other people behave differently, *should* you be able to cope better, and *should* this not be happening to you?

Summing Up

- You will never know when sudden stress is going to strike – you could have a car accident, an unexpected row, some dreadful news or reach the end of your tether.

- By knowing what steps to take, you can help yourself out of stressful situations or you may be able to help someone else who is suffering.

- A long-term approach to stress is also necessary to cope with whatever happens to you in your life.

- The more that you can develop a lifestyle in which you look after your health and wellbeing and adopt a calmer attitude, the more you will be able to face the inevitable difficulties that everyone has to encounter.

Chapter Four

Your Own Worst Enemy?

Stress begets stress – if you feel stressed everything else becomes difficult. It is much harder to cope with relationship problems if your work life is problematic. Sometimes you can find yourself becoming extremely stressed about small things because the big things aren't right.

There are numerous ways that you can cause your own stress. Some of the reasons are:

※ Your belief systems.

※ Judgements you make.

※ Perfectionism.

※ Procrastination.

※ Not wanting to face things.

Take a look at the following questions and find out how many you answer yes to.

Could you be your own worst enemy?

※ Do you feel guilty if you take time to relax?

※ Do you find it hard to ask for help – at work, with the children or with anything?

※ Do you commit yourself even though you don't want to do something?

※ Do you wallow in situations without making changes?

※ Do you fail to communicate how you feel?

※ Are you doing things to please someone else, but not being true to yourself?

- Do you find it hard to spend time alone without the TV or radio on?
- Do you feel as if you never have any time?
- Do you prefer to do things for yourself because you do them best?
- Do you make yourself do things that make life more difficult for you?

If you answer yes to three or four of these you may be your own worst enemy.

Why some people are affected more than others

People vary as to what stresses them and often there are things that you will find very stressful and others don't – and vice versa. How you respond to stressors may depend on any of the following:

- Childhood experience.
- Personality type.
- Self-esteem and confidence.
- Inherited response.
- Illness which weakens stress resilience.
- Tendency towards depression.
- General health and wellbeing – diet and exercise.

The worst scenario is when a number of very stressful events happen either in succession or at the same time. If you are subjected to three or four of the main stressors, for instance, bereavement, divorce and losing your job all in the same period, it is highly likely that you will feel extremely stressed.

The effects of illness

You are more likely to get stressed when you are ill because you do not have the energy to cope with problems. It is a vicious circle – stress makes you more likely to succumb to illness and being unwell makes you less able to cope.

Even having flu for two weeks can make you feel as if you are out of control and that everything is getting on top of you. Serious illness is even more difficult to deal with and if you or someone close to you is dying it may feel very unfair.

Trying to accept what is happening rather than denying it, can alleviate some of the stress on you, but this is not always easy to do. Death is an inevitable fact of life, but many of us struggle with coming to terms with it.

Try to look after yourself emotionally (whether you are the person who is ill or it is someone close to you). Speaking to a close friend, a religious leader, or a counsellor can be helpful, and take time out to relax and be looked after as well. (See chapters 9 and 11).

Causing your own stress

Have a long think about who is causing your stress. You might like to choose from the following:

- A friend.

- A parent or other family member.

- A partner.

- Your son or daughter.

- Your boss or other work colleagues.

- A particular situation.

- A neighbour.

- Or you?

It can often be easier to blame someone or something else for how you feel, but it helps to see what part you are playing in your own problems.

Even though you may feel that someone else is causing you stress, is it possible that it is you? By your own reaction to what they are saying or doing, you may be stressing yourself. You can't always influence external factors, but you can influence your perceptions, thoughts and values.

Taking responsibility

If you genuinely feel that someone else is causing your stress, you need to start taking control of your life. Ask yourself if your partner or someone else in your life makes decisions that affect you without consulting you. Do you abdicate responsibility and let them decide everything in the belief that you are easy-going?

If you have given responsibility for your life to someone else, it is likely that you will feel resentful and out of control – if not now, at a later stage. Maybe you feel that you find it too stressful to make your own decisions. If you take back responsibility for your own life, you are likely to feel more in control and better about yourself.

You may be fairly convinced that someone else is causing your stress, but blaming others can make you feel even worse. Only you are responsible for your feelings, so ask yourself the question, 'How would it be if I didn't feel like this?'

Step back from the situation and try to examine your own feelings objectively. You could look at what has happened and decide that the stress is all being caused in your own head – this gives back the control to you as you choose how to deal with it.

Making judgements

Having a pre-conceived idea of how everything and everyone should be, can cause considerable stress. You may want your partner or children to behave in a certain way, but they don't!

Believing that things should be a certain way can cause considerable disappointment and make you put a lot of pressure on yourself.

Do you ever tell yourself, 'I should be able to cope with this'? If you are not coping well this adds extra pressure and it would be better if you were kind to yourself. Even admitting, 'I find this difficult to handle' would be better than chastising yourself.

Need2Know

Belief systems

It can be hard to negate your own belief systems because they may have been drummed into you since you were very little.

For example:

- You may have been brought up to believe that you have to succeed in your career.
- You may have a strong belief that marriage is for life and that divorce is wrong.
- Since childhood you might have felt inadequate, with low self-esteem.
- You may believe that people don't like you.

Realising that your belief systems might be working against you could be a first step to easing stress on yourself. It's not possible to change such deeply held beliefs overnight, but by reading this book you will find ways to help yourself.

What if?

Do you find yourself worrying about things that might never happen?

For example:

- What if my partner leaves me?
- What if I lose my job?
- What if my children don't grow up how I want them to?
- What if I become seriously ill?
- What if my friend doesn't invite me round?

You create your own reality in your head. If you worry about something enough it can become a self-fulfilling prophecy and actually happen.

If you could reach the stage of believing that you can cope in any situation, you wouldn't need to worry so much.

'Realising that your belief systems might be working against you could be a first step to easing stress on yourself. It's not possible to change such deeply held beliefs overnight, but by reading this book you will find ways to help yourself.'

Procrastination

Sometimes a job you have put off doing for months only takes 10 minutes. Yet you have spent months worrying yourself that it needs to be done.

The more things you put off today, the more you pile up problems for the future. Then when they all catch up with you, they are much more stressful than if you'd handled them at the time. On the other hand, if you deal with tasks as they arise you will get a sense of satisfaction from having achieved or completed them.

This may not just apply to chores and jobs, but may involve talking to someone about something or making major changes in your life.

Untidiness

Untidy people are sometimes perfectionists – they cannot clear up until they have time to do it properly.

Clearing the clutter out of your life can help to clear your brain as well. If you are surrounded by mounds of paper or untidy rooms full of junk, it's hard to feel focused and relaxed. Making order out of chaos can feel very fulfilling.

Perfectionism

Perfectionism spills over into all areas of life. Here are some examples:

- You can't relax unless the house is spotless.

- You cannot go out unless you are totally happy with your appearance.

- No one else can do anything as well as you, so you may as well do it.

- You must be indispensable in every area of your life.

- Because you don't do something perfectly (like play a sport) you don't bother at all.

Just because other people may seem to be supermen or women, don't judge yourself by them – chances are they're not nearly as super as you think. You do not need to impose deadlines on yourself and get annoyed when you don't meet them. Recognise what you are capable of and that you are an individual and it doesn't matter what other people do or think.

Pleasing others

Little girls start young in wanting to please others, particularly their mothers. This often extends into adult life and is in some way part and parcel of being a wife and mother. You often see it as your role to keep everyone happy, without recognising that everyone is responsible for themselves (when they are old enough).

It's great to be nice and helpful to people, but if you are doing it because of a need to be liked, it may not be serving you that well. If you are pleasing others by helping them it can make you feel good about yourself, but if you do too much of it, you can become stressed out.

Saying no

Both men and women are guilty of not saying no enough. Whether it's in the workplace, home or social life, a lot of people find that they are unable to say no to anyone.

If you are being put upon and being asked to do extra work, to pick up other people's children too regularly, to visit people you don't want to see, or you are treated like a dogsbody at home, it is time to say no.

There is no point in agreeing to things you don't want to do if it stresses you out and makes you fed up. Just saying no in itself is not rude, if you say it nicely – 'I'm really sorry but I can't help you out today.' Children need to know that you aren't their servant and that you are entitled to a life too!

'Just because other people may seem to be supermen or women, don't judge yourself by them – chances are they're not nearly as super as you think. You do not need to impose deadlines on yourself and get annoyed when you don't meet them. Recognise what you are capable of and that you are an individual and it doesn't matter what other people do or think.'

Guilt

One of the reasons why saying no is so hard is because of guilt which often drives us into doing things we don't want to do, and is frequently the cause of stress.

The feeling that you 'ought' to do something because you feel guilty can in itself be stressful, so you can take the easy way out and do it – but it's not always the easy way out!

Ask yourself:

- Do I feel guilty if I spend time relaxing?
- Do I feel guilty if I make time to exercise?
- Who do I feel guilty towards?
- Is it myself?
- Why?

'Better to complete a small task well, than to do much imperfectly'.
Plato.

Being assertive means saying how you feel without being rude or aggressive. There are many short assertiveness courses available that give you the chance to role play and say what you mean so that it is understood and taken without offence.

Taking on too much

Nowadays, many people expect to have it all. This particularly applies to women who work and bring up children, but men can experience it too. Add to this being the social secretary for the family, running the home, doing the housework and paying the bills, and there doesn't seem much time left.

Try this exercise – write down how many things you have done in a day. Include everything, like emptying the dishwasher, going to the shops, walking the dog, picking up the children, doing a day's work. See how many it adds up to.

If you are feeling very stressed you need to ask yourself which of these things you could get someone else to do or which you could dispense with. You may not want to stop seeing your friends, but maybe you could go out for a meal, get a takeaway or cook something simple instead of a three-course cordon bleu extravaganza.

Ask yourself if it is really necessary to do this now, and give yourself a break. Try to get some balance in your life – there are always tasks to be completed, but don't drive yourself too much.

Get your priorities straight

The choices we make are what cause much of our stress.

Buddhism focuses on living in the now, rather than in the past or future, and puts total emphasis on personal growth, not on material gain. Remember what really matters in life – are you putting work or less important things above your family? Think of your priorities and put them first.

Learn to be patient with yourself and others, and forgive yourself for your imperfections, weaknesses and fragility. Just accepting them is the first step to changing.

'Learn to be patient with yourself and others, and forgive yourself for your imperfections, weaknesses and fragility. Just accepting them is the first step to changing.'

Summing Up

■ It isn't the stressful events that adversely affect people, but how they deal with them. Some people respond negatively to any problem, whereas others try to see the positive in most situations.

■ A lot of people don't seem to do themselves any favours by their own behaviour patterns. For instance, you may be a perfectionist, have problems saying no, be motivated by guilt, procrastinate or allow other people to run your life for you.

■ There are many things that you can do to make life easier for yourself if you let some of your normal habits drop and decide to treat yourself kindly.

Chapter Five

The 21st Century Workplace

There couldn't be a worse time for work stress than now, when the economic climate is at its worst and showing no sign of improving. It is a long time ago that anyone could expect a 'job for life'. Instead, what many people have to put up with is a climate of uncertainty, never knowing if they will have a job for long. Or if they are self-employed they may be wondering whether business will ever pick up.

Work stress has been in the news a lot due to the current economic situation. Many companies are struggling and staff are concerned about their job security, and may feel unmotivated and at worse ill with stress and stress-related conditions.

While this chapter looks at the effects of stress in the workplace and what measures companies are employing to improve its effect on absence levels, chapter 6, Work-Life Balance, looks at how individuals can help themselves in the workplace.

The vicious circle

A government-funded report into work and relationships in Britain carried out by the Working Families and One Plus One charities, found that business downsizing, long working hours and job insecurity are the norm, meaning that people are more and more stressed and feel that they are missing out on family life because of long hours. Some 86% of working parents feel that they have lost out on time with their children.

Effectively, it means that people have the worst of both worlds – more and more work to get through but often with a threat that they may lose their jobs however hard they work. The preliminary findings of this study found that 25% of workers do more than their contracted hours, with only 7% never working extra hours.

It seems that the stress of work is causing a health hazard in many ways too, with one third of people blaming it for excessive smoking and drinking, and half of those questioned sacrificing regular exercise as a direct result. As many as 1/3 of employees suffer from anxiety or panic attacks because of work stress.

Nearly one third of those questioned in the two-year Happy Homes, Productive Workplaces project, felt less productive and less engaged. About the same number were distracted at work due to stress at home, so work stress is affecting family life, and family stress is affecting work.

Stress causes long-term absence

Stress is now the number one cause of long-term absence, according to the Chartered Institute of Personnel Development (CIPD) and Simplyhealth Absence Management Survey in 2011. It affects both manual and non-manual employees and the main causes of stress at work were found to be:

- Heavy workloads.
- Management style.
- Relationships at work.
- Organisational change and restructuring.
- External factors – relationships at home.

According to the Absence Management Survey, 60% of organisations are taking steps to identify and reduce stress in the workplace. As in previous years, public service employers are most likely to be proactively managing stress but the proportion doing so has fallen in comparison with previous years.

The elephant in the room

The mental health charity, Mind, surveyed 2,050 workers in 2010 and found that nearly 20% of them had phoned in sick because of unmanageable stress levels. In most cases they had lied about why they were feeling unwell and blamed a stomach bug or headache rather than admit the truth – long hours, excessive workloads or bullying. Mind describes mental health at work as 'the elephant in the room'.

The charity launched a five-year campaign called 'Taking Care of Business' to improve the wellbeing of workers in the UK by challenging stigma, bullying and inadequate support services at work. They believe that businesses will benefit by acknowledging mental health issues, rather than sweeping them under the carpet.

Health and Safety Executive (HSE) research shows that stress accounts for half of all working days lost each year, costing employers £26 billion a year. When people are stressed they are likely to have symptoms like poor concentration, low motivation and tiredness, which makes them less productive.

Further research showed that HR directors did not believe that any of their employees suffered from a mental health problem. The aim of the Taking Care of Business campaign is to help and encourage employers to be more open about mental health issues such as stress. One of the first aims of Mind is to ensure that people take their hour's lunch break

Mind presented compelling new evidence that the economic crisis has had a devastating effect on the wellbeing of British workers. The charity has found that since the downturn:

- 1 in 11 workers have sought support from their doctors.

- 7% have started taking medication, such as antidepressants, for stress and mental health problems directly caused by the pressures of recession on their workplace.

The findings, which launch Mind's campaign 'Taking Care of Business' (www.mind.org.uk/employment), coincide with new government statistics showing: The biggest rise in antidepressant prescriptions ever, with a record 39.1 million issued in 2009, up from 35.9 million in 2008.

For manual workers, stress is at the same level as acute medical conditions for reasons of absence, but it is now higher than musculoskeletal problems which used to be top of the list. For non-manual staff, stress is ahead of acute medical conditions.

Job security has had a detrimental effect on mental health problems too. Where employers were expecting to make redundancies in the next six months, there were more staff (51%) suffering from mental health problems, as opposed to only 32% in companies not planning redundancies.

Stress-related absence has become particularly prevalent in public sector organisations, with half of them reporting an increase. The reasons for this were cited as, principally, the high amount of organisational change and restructuring, as well as the impact of cuts to jobs, pension benefits and pay freezes.

Absence levels

Each employee in the Absence Management Survey has an average of 7.7 days absent each year, with public sector absence going down by 0.5% to 9.1 days per person per year. Private sector absence has jumped from 6.6 days in 2010, to 7.1 days in 2011.

The lowest levels of absence are among manufacturing and production organisations, while non-profit organisations had the highest. Colds, flu, headaches and stomach upsets account for most days off for short-term absence, and rate higher than stress.

How companies deal with stress

When employees become more stressed due to job insecurity, they are less productive and more likely to be absent from work. The survey found that half of the employers they surveyed had a wellbeing strategy in place, with as many as 73% of the companies providing counselling services, and nearly 70% providing an Employee Assistance Programme. Both these services enable staff to discuss workplace issues, as well as emotional and psychological problems.

The Absence Management Survey found that the approach of an organisation to its employees' absence and attendance can have a significant impact, not just on absence levels but also on business efficiency and performance.

The 2011 Absence Management Survey report is based on 592 valid responses to an online survey questionnaire. The survey comprised of 40 questions exploring absence levels, causes and costs, as well as how organisations attempt to manage absence and promote health and wellbeing at work and the impact of the economic climate on employee absence rates.

The full report can be read at:

www.cipd.co.uk/hr-resources/survey-reports/absence-management-2011.aspx

---

Work stress affects heart health of under 50 year old women

A study of more than 12,000 women nurses aged from 45 to 64 found that more of them under 50 suffered from heart disease due to work stress than those over 50. The researchers asked the nurses about pressure at work and tracked their health for 15 years up until 2008. By this time 580 of the nurses had been admitted to hospital with heart disease, including 369 cases of angina and 138 heart attacks.

The researchers looked at risk factors such as smoking and diabetes and found that those who considered their work pressure was 'much too high' had a 35% greater chance of developing heart disease than those who felt comfortable with the pressure. It turned out that only the women under 50 were significantly affected.

The research was carried out at Glostrup University Hospital, Denmark.

Stress may prompt other illnesses

In recent years there has been a considerable increase in the amount of workplace schemes aimed at tackling stress. This is not just an altruistic measure, but the need for companies to reduce absence levels in a very difficult economic climate is crucial.

Although work stress is a major problem, when employees take time off due to stress they don't always say what is wrong with them, preferring to cite other illnesses instead, such as upset stomachs, headaches, and back pain.

On the other hand, many illnesses are actually caused by stress and so are really stress-related illnesses. This is not necessarily easy to prove, but it is well known that someone who is stressed is more likely to be susceptible to illness, such as stomach problems, headaches and back pain. Feelings of unhappiness can predispose someone to more serious illness too and many serious health issues may appear to have started during stressful periods.

The economic downturn has brought about a slowing down among companies implementing stress-reduction strategies, even though they need to reduce absence to improve their performance. The majority of companies who do take measures to deal with stress seem to consider that counselling is the most effective way of helping their employees.

Stress-reduction strategies include some of the following:

- Counselling or CBT (cognitive behavioural therapy).
- Training of staff, especially managers, on how to deal with work stress.
- Mentoring and staff surveys.
- Work-life balance policies including flexible working hours.
- Employee assistance programmes.
- Subsidised or free relaxation classes and/or complementary therapies (such as massage).

In difficult times companies might consider cutting back on some of these benefits, but conversely, because they need to keep absence levels low, this is the time when the schemes are needed most of all. It is, however, possible that any companies that were considering putting in stress-reduction programmes may be less inclined to while times are hard.

Summing up

- Stress is really taking its toll in the workplace, with a culture of insecurity due to the threat of job losses.

- There is a vicious circle, in that people are spending more time working because they are worried about losing their jobs, but they are also missing out on family life.

- Companies have recognised that they need to implement strategies to help people to cope with stress, not least because such schemes usually improve absence levels.

Chapter Six

Work–Life Balance

The UK has the longest working hours in Europe, and is the only EU country that has allowed staff to opt out of the maximum 48 hour week set by the Working Time Directive.

One in six workers works more than 60 hours a week and 29% of employees with high stress levels work more than 10 hours longer than they are contracted to do, according to a survey conducted by the Department of Trade and Industry's Work-Life Balance Campaign and the magazine, *Management Today*.

You might be lucky and work for a company that looks after its employees and has introduced flexible working hours, home working, or even access to stress management, relaxation and exercise classes.

The technological revolution

Computers may have revolutionised the office but they have increased workloads. All but the chief executive (and sometimes him or her too) do their own emails and create documents for themselves, adding hugely to their workload.

Blackberries, mobile phones and laptops mean that you can be in touch with work at any time of the day, wherever you are, even on holiday. As for emails, they have become the bane of most people's working lives, with huge amounts of junk mail and extra time in the day required to respond to the non-junk.

'For every hour that you work over seven, you compromise your efficiency by five minutes per hour. But people don't notice this, nor do they believe it.' Professor Ben Fletcher, Professor of Personal and Organisational Development and Head of School, the University of Hertfordshire.

'For every hour that you work over seven, you compromise your efficiency by five minutes per hour. But people don't notice this, nor do they believe it.'

Professor Ben Fletcher, Professor of Personal and Organisational Development and Head of Psychology School, the University of Hertfordshire.

The most common causes of stress in the workplace

There are two types of stress in the workplace – that which is imposed from the culture of the company or from your superiors, or that which is self-imposed.

Some imposed causes

- High job demands with pressure from above on productivity and performance.
- The obsession with targets (as in the health service).
- Low pay or reward – not being paid a reasonable rate for the job, or being asked to do more than should be reasonably expected for the amount paid.
- Bullying and harassment (sexual or racist) from colleagues or bosses.
- Not enough work to do and not feeling valued.
- Being given boring and repetitive work, which does not take account of your abilities.
- No prospects of furthering your career.
- Poor working conditions – bad lighting, noisy, dirty, run-down buildings or cramped workspaces.
- A culture of blame or passing the buck.
- Working with people who are unprofessional and expect you to compromise your standards.
- Lack of control, consultation or communication.

It is essential to keep a sense of perspective about work and remember that there are always other jobs out there. You may be tempted by high salaries, but if your health is suffering is it worth it?

Unless you have made a positive choice for it to do so, your job should not take over your life. If you are worrying about it all the time you are not at work, something is wrong. No job is worth your life.

Is your job stressing you out?

- Do you feel pressured to meet deadlines or productivity targets?

- Is anyone at work bullying you or harassing you, sexually or otherwise?

- Do you feel that unreasonable demands are being made on you at work?

- Do you work more than 40 hours a week?

- Is there a climate of uncertainty about redundancies or sacking in your workplace?

- Is the organisation cutting costs by slimming down the workforce?

- Are you doing work that used to be carried out by a number of other people?

- Do bosses/superiors leave you out of decision-making that concerns you?

- Do they ignore, overlook or not deal effectively with complaints and conflicts?

- Are you left to sort problems out yourself, without sufficient back up?

If you answer yes to only one of the above you might be feeling stressed by work, but if the answer is yes to three or more, it is highly likely that your stress levels are high.

How to help yourself at work

- Working late: try to avoid working late every day, even if it is company culture.

- Delegate or ask for help: don't believe you're indispensable, and if you're worried about something it is better to ask than do it incorrectly or ignore it altogether.

- Take lunch breaks: get out of the workplace, go for a walk, have something to eat, or meet a friend so that you can switch off for half an hour to an hour.

- Communicate: find out who the best person is to discuss problems with, or ask if you can be moved into a different department if colleagues or your boss are difficult to work with. If everyone is stressed out, perhaps several of you can ask for changes to be made.

- Be honest: if you always get stressed in every job you do, perhaps there is a pattern developing due to your own way of doing things. It may not be the fault of the job.

Heavy workloads

Make a plan for the week setting out what you will do each day. By breaking work up into chunks it feels more manageable.

Dealing with emails

- Sort through junk quickly and daily.

- Put a coloured flag on important ones.

- Allocate some time in the day to deal with non-urgent ones.

- Don't check your email box too often or you will be tempted to get involved.

- Turn off your email program while working so email does not keep popping up and distracting you.

Unrealistic deadlines and promises

- Don't procrastinate – get on with what needs doing.

- Learn to say '*No*'.

- If you feel that you are not going to be able to meet a deadline say so within good time – you may be given longer.

- If you are really worried about letting people down, communicate your problem and ask for help.

- Try to maintain a sense of perspective and a sense of humour.

Meetings

Some companies have a meetings culture, which inevitably means that people spend a lot of time just talking things over and over, or, at worst, chatting socially! One advertising agency took away its tables and chairs in the meeting rooms, did not serve coffee and found that meetings lasted five or ten minutes.

- If you have any influence at all, try to cut down on meetings.
- Ask if it could be done on the phone or by email.
- Could a short report be written instead?
- If people are going to travel a long way to an hour's meeting they may be pleased to avoid it.

You can then spend more time doing the work you are supposed to be doing.

Outside work

The more you earn the more you are expected to be available outside working hours. The pressure put on you may come from your bosses, but many people put it on themselves, believing that they are indispensable.

If you have the kind of boss who wants to spend hours discussing things on the weekend, turn off your mobile phone when you are away from work. Make it clear that when you are on holiday you are not going to be contactable and leave your laptop at home. (If you own the company this might not be possible).

Workaholics abound

You don't have to be an employee to be a workaholic. Many self-employed people work non-stop. This may be because they are a one-man band and haven't got anyone to help them, or because it's hard to get away from the work because it's at their home.

Extra discipline has to apply in this situation because it is you who dictates your hours of work. Shut the door on work, have rules about when you don't work – no work on Saturdays for example, and take holidays away from home.

Are you a workaholic?

- Is work the most important thing in your life?
- Do you take work home?
- Do you think about work when you are at home or out socially?
- If you had to leave work in the next month or so, do you have an alternative?
- Do you feel that no one else can do the job as well as you do?
- If you are ill are you averse to taking time off?
- Do you always have extra days' holiday entitlement left over at the end of the year?
- Do you regularly work more than eight hours a day?
- Do you work more than 48 hours a week?

Of course you may feel that work is your life and you love it, and without it your life would be stressful. These questions are for people who are feeling very stressed by their work and who are blaming the job.

Questions for the workaholic:

- Is your self-esteem bound up in your career/job?
- Do you feel that you need to prove yourself?
- Do you have a fear of failure?
- Are you avoiding something else in your life – your family for instance?
- Are you lonely and does work give you a purpose?
- Does it make you feel important?
- Are you trying to make up for the past – failing your GCSEs or 11+?
- Does working make you feel in control?

'Workaholics are often perfectionist, obsessive personalities, while sham workaholics stay late in order to be seen to be working hard – witness the boss who stays from 7 to 10 every day.'

Professor Ben Fletcher, University of Hertfordshire.

The effect on your health

Stress in the workplace affects performance of the brain, work performance, memory, concentration and learning. In the year 2006 to 2007 according to HSE figures, self-reported work-related illness indicated that 530,000 people in the UK believed that they were experiencing work-related stress at a level that was making them ill.

The Quality of Working Life report published by the Chartered Management Institute and Workplace Health Connect of 1,541 managers found:

- 43% became angry with people too easily.

- 1/3 experienced loss of humour, creating workplace pressures.

- 55% said they had muscular tension.

- 44% had headaches.

- 55% complained of constant tiredness.

- 57% suffered from insomnia.

What can you do about a stressful environment?

- If you have genuine grievances at work such as bullying, harassment – sexual or otherwise – low pay, poor health and safety conditions or similar situations, you need to make a formal complaint.

- Find out if there is a proper procedure for making complaints, airing grievances or explaining how stress is affecting you – if there is a union, speak to a representative.

- Talk to a supervisor, manager or anyone senior to you, unless they are causing your problem, in which case find out who else you could see.

- If you need help ask for it from whoever can help you – whatever their position.

- Discreetly talk to colleagues who may feel the same.

'While they think they are more efficient and feel fine, empirical studies demonstrate that working too much affects performance, mental wellbeing, physical wellbeing, constrains vision and decision-making ability, making people narrow focused.'

Professor Ben Fletcher.

If things don't improve

- Weigh up the pros and cons and decide if you can stay and accept the situation but learn not to get stressed out by it.

- Find another job within the organisation or elsewhere.

- Look at the options for flexible working, part-time working or job share.

- See if the company would allow you to work from home or be freelance and not work for them all the time.

If all else fails, you need to consider leaving. There are always other jobs out there. And if you're worried about your age, in theory employers can no longer discriminate on age since the introduction of the Age Discrimination Act in October 2006. You may find a company where the culture is much better and more enjoyable.

Getting help

Health and Safety Executive (HSE), responsible for health and safety regulations in UK businesses. Call the HSE Info Line 0845 345 0055 or visit www.hse.gov.uk.

Employment Tribunals, call the public enquiry line on 0845 795 9775, which is open from 9am to 5pm, Monday to Friday, or visit www.employmenttribunals. gov.uk.

Advisory, Conciliation and Arbitration Service (ACAS), call 08457 474747, Monday to Friday, 8am-8pm, or visit www.acas.org.uk . ACAS provides free e-learning packages for individuals on subjects including bullying and harassment, age discrimination, managing absence and working parents.

Work-Life Balance Centre, call 01530 273056 or visit www. worklifebalancecentre.org. This organisation provides information and research about stress at work.

Business Balls, visit www.businessballs.com/stressmanagement.htm. This is a helpful website with lots of tips and information about handling stress at work.

Summing Up

■ Today's working environment is often stressful and there are a lot of organisations where the culture is not conducive to employees' health and wellbeing.

■ Companies are encouraged to take stress seriously as part of their risk management strategy, and consider their employees' wellbeing as vital to the success of the organisation – which is, after all, only as good as the people in it.

■ It is possible that you exacerbate the situation by pressuring yourself, or maybe you are a workaholic.

■ A job should not rule your life and if it does you need to keep a sense of perspective – you can always leave.

Chapter Seven

You Deserve the Best

Take action for a better life

As life is always going to be stressful, it helps to have an approach that enables you to cope. Waiting for stress to go away doesn't work well because there's always more waiting in the wings.

Finding a philosophy to help you cope with life's ups and downs is the best bet. Adopting the Buddhist philosophy of living in the now – the past is over and the future may not happen (certainly not how you have already planned it) – can make for an easier life. If you can learn to take each day at a time it pays dividends, but it also takes a lot of practice!

Some self-help strategies

Tackle problems individually

Sometimes things seem to keep going wrong and you feel overwhelmed. One way to deal with this is to tackle problems as they arise individually – if you can. Try to rationalise how serious they are, not turning them all into disasters.

Getting a sense of perspective

Every day there are scenes on television of people starving or dying, and for most people this is more stressful than their everyday life. If you were fighting for your very survival, many of the things that concern you now would not be so important, yet it's often hard to see it that way when you're stressed.

'Finding a philosophy to help you cope with life's major ups and downs is the best bet. Adopting the Buddhist philosophy of living in the now – the past is over and the future may not happen (certainly not how you have already planned it) – can make for an easier life. If you can learn to take each day at a time it pays dividends, but it also takes a lot of practice!'

Try to see the good in any situation

This can seem the most absurd suggestion when you are feeling overwhelmed by the loss of someone close or something equally as devastating. Certainly some people would feel that you were trivialising their problems if you said it. Nevertheless, when you look back you can see how the biggest problems of your life have shaped and matured you.

Treat others as individuals

It's quite usual for people to live their lives through their children, but when this comes to doggedly sticking to your aspirations and desires for them, you sometimes overlook your children's needs and desires. Trying to get someone else to change or do what you want them to do is a great source of stress, so practise letting go.

Learn to face rejection

The most stressful events usually have other impacts in your life – if your marriage or long-term relationship breaks up there are many implications for your life and those of your children if you have them. Once you move on to meet someone else or enjoy the single life you can look back and see what was wrong with the relationship.

Try to be philosophical – maybe it wasn't meant to be.

See *Divorce and Separation – The Essential Guide* (Need2Know) for more information.

Take action

One of the best ways of dealing with rejection is to take action. If your partner has left you, invite a friend over, arrange a trip or take up a new sport or hobby. If you've lost your job, you could think about retraining, if you can afford it. You could consider being self-employed, sort out your garden or start looking for the kind of job you really want.

Be realistic

Don't go through life pretending or hoping it will never happen to you. Develop strategies for dealing with stressful events and plan for the future. Start to believe that you will cope with what you have to, rather than dreading it and hoping it will never happen.

Don't make a drama out of a crisis

How many times have you become stressed about something that you thought had happened or was going to happen and it turned out to be alright? It happens all the time, but if you wait until you know the full facts and try not to think the worst, it could save you some anguish!

Be organised, but not perfect

Keeping your papers and bills up to date, your house tidy and your finances in order makes life much easier. It means that when a crisis arises you haven't got a lot of extra problems to worry about as well. But try not to be too perfect – if you haven't done something it's not worth beating yourself up about it.

Live authentically

If you are true to yourself many areas of your life will take care of themselves – you can say no when you want to and you won't get into situations that you regret or dislike. Being honest with everyone, including yourself, usually makes life easier, provided you do it in the most appropriate way.

Boost your memory

Losing anything can make you feel out of control, frustrated and angry and it can be a great time-waster. Try to be kind to yourself. Here are a few self-help hints:

- Put your keys in the same place every day – hang them on a hook or put them in a bowl when you walk into the house.

'The level of unhappiness in your life equals the size of the lie you are living.'
Caroline Reynolds, author of *Spiritual Fitness*.

- Buy a notebook and write messages or phone numbers down in it rather than writing them on pieces of paper or trying to remember them!

- Write lists and notes to remind you of dates, appointments, and what you need to do.

- Put things away consciously – repeat to yourself, 'I have put the tickets in my wallet' and then you will remember.

- Take the herbal remedy ginkgo if your memory is really bad – it increases circulation to the brain. (Check with a medical herbalist or GP if you are taking medication).

- Keep a diary and a calendar so you can remind yourself of important dates – don't try and remember in your head or leave them in a file on your PC.

Save time

'I don't think of the past. The only thing that matters is the everlasting present.'

Somerset Maugham.

Think about your time management. We all waste time doing things we do and don't want to do. Nowadays there is a completely new time-waster – surfing the Internet, which is costing companies many hours of productive time.

If you are a full-time carer and you genuinely have little or no time to yourself, see if you can call upon social services or charities in your area to give you a much-needed break as often as possible.

Make contingency plans

At the back of your mind you can have a plan for what you will do if your job doesn't work out. If you have already given it some thought it helps you to cope if you are made redundant.

Enjoy your children

They'll be grown up before you can think about it, and at some stage in their teens they won't want to do things with you – they might not even speak to you! Enjoy them while they are young and spend as much time as you can with them so you don't regret it later on.

Being good to yourself

You are your own best asset, so take care of yourself. Don't do things for other people that you feel are wrong, and allow yourself time to relax and enjoy life. If you look after others all the time, you need you to be fit and well so make sure you look after yourself.

Communication is key

You may think you communicate but it is a two-way thing – it means saying how you feel as well as listening to other's feelings too. When you communicate effectively it is so much easier to get on with people and to have them understand what your problems are.

For example, if you let your mother down for the third time in a row she might be upset and annoyed. If you explain what is happening to you and the problems you are facing, and that your car is playing up and it's snowing outside, she is more likely to understand.

Nurture your relationships

Life is much easier to face if you have people whom you love and who love you. Relationships need nurturing and communication because they don't automatically take care of themselves.

We all have ups and downs and one week you may feel you want to run off with the man or woman you've seen at the gym, but the next week you're quite contented. This is quite normal, but it's not normal if you think about nothing else. It may be that your relationship has problems that need to be looked at, or you might have your priorities wrong.

Try to talk to your partner about problems as they arise and be honest with each other. If you know you're not in a good relationship you might benefit from going to see a Relate counsellor to talk it through – you can see them alone or as a couple. (See the help list.)

Plan fun things to do

Having fun need not be expensive – if you can't afford much, what about going to the cinema, for a walk or inviting a friend over for a coffee? If funds aren't too much of a problem, have a weekend away, book the theatre or a concert, or have people round to dinner.

Make life easier

If you are very busy all the time, can you consider having your shopping delivered? It costs £5 or less and you save that much in petrol or parking. Or find someone to do some cleaning, gardening or dog walking for you if you can afford it. Suggest to another parent that you start a rota for school runs, so that you don't have to drive (or walk) to school every morning and afternoon.

Good friends

A good friend can be in your life for many years and is always there when you need them. Friends can share your joys and sorrows, lend a helping hand and be a great source of comfort and enjoyment. Just keeping in touch by email or phone can be good enough.

There are people who make you smile and laugh, and it's certainly good for your wellbeing and stress levels to see the funny side of life. However bad things have become, try to spend some time with people you enjoy seeing and who help you to relax.

Furry companions

There may be people you love, and they may not be people at all. There is now something called pet therapy where cats and dogs are taken to see seriously ill people to give them some pleasure. If you have pets you'll know how comforting they can be – cats can teach humans something about learning to relax, and dogs can be fun and they keep you active.

'There are people who make you smile and laugh, and it's certainly good for your wellbeing and stress levels to see the funny side of life. However bad things have become, try to spend some time with people you enjoy seeing and who help you to relax.'

Go on holiday

Some people don't take holidays because they say they cannot afford them or because they don't have enough time.

It doesn't have to be expensive to take a break. Even if you took a week off work and visited some local places you've never been to it wouldn't be costly, but it can be relaxing.

Sing

Yes, sing – to yourself or take it up seriously. Here are a few reasons why it's good for you:

- Releases chemicals in the brain and body.
- Distracts you from stress, releases tension and provides relief.
- Warms and relaxes muscles, enabling you to relax.
- It's fun and enjoyable and allows you to let go.
- It gives you confidence.

The answer is in your hands

Do you ever think that life would be better if you had:

- A new partner?
- A new job?
- Left home?
- Earned more money?
- Moved to a new country?
- Grown-up children?

Stop blaming other people or situations for why you're not happy. You alone are the only person who can make your own happiness.

Summing Up

- There is much you can do to make your life easier, but changes do not happen overnight.

- Taking responsibility for yourself and your actions means that you are more in control, rather than blaming other people.

- You may have no control at all about the stress that is imposed upon you. If, however, you are happy with your life and the people in it, it gives you a stronger base from which to cope with difficulties that come along.

- If you understand yourself and your reactions, you are also in a better position to handle problems.

- Look after yourself by surrounding yourself with people or even pets who you love, and activities that you enjoy.

Chapter Eight

Sort Your Life Out

There are some people who can make positive changes in their life by simple willpower or because events have changed them. You may find it more helpful to have some professional help – counselling, life coaching or other kinds of therapy are all helpful.

You may not automatically make a connection between stress and your self-esteem, but learning to cope with what life throws at you is easier if you feel confident and believe in yourself. You are the worst critic you will ever have, so maybe it's time to start being kinder to yourself!

You may find that when you think about it you are not very forgiving of your mistakes and that you do not accept who you are, and that you (like everyone else) are not perfect. Working on your self-esteem is a very valid way to make yourself stronger and more resilient to life's stresses.

Counselling

Even though counselling is much more widely accepted these days, there are still people who believe that you must have something 'wrong' with you if you need therapy. In fact it is often a sign of strength to see a therapist, and it can help you to get life in perspective and manage stress more effectively.

There are various different types of counselling and psychotherapies, but the recent term 'talking therapy' is perhaps most appropriate. Seeing a counsellor or psychotherapist gives you the opportunity to talk in confidence to someone who is completely uninvolved emotionally.

'You may not automatically make a connection between stress and your self-esteem, but learning to cope with what life throws at you is easier if you feel confident and believe in yourself. You are the worst critic you will ever have, so maybe it's time to start being kinder to yourself!'

Counsellors are trained to listen and to help you find your own truth, so that you become more aware of what makes you tick and what has happened in your life that has made you the way you are. It can be a very positive experience leading to greater contentment, personal growth and development.

Most people who see a counsellor have relationship problems, emotional problems or they may be feeling depressed or unable to cope with life. For anyone who has serious mental health problems, it is more appropriate for the GP to refer them to a psychiatrist.

Counselling is available on the NHS but it is usually limited to six sessions, which, although they are free, might not always be enough for you. If money is a concern some of these organisations are charities and will take ability to pay into account. They are listed in the help list at the back of the book.

If you have relationship problems you may want to go for couples' counselling either with a private counsellor or to Relate who ask for a donation. If you have been bereaved it is helpful to go to Cruse counsellors. There are also various organisations for specific problems, such as people suffering from cancer.

British Association for Counselling and Psychotherapy, call 0870 443 5252 or visit www.bacp.co.uk.

Cruse Bereavement Care, call 0844 477 9400 or visit www.cruse.org.uk.

Relate, call 0300 100 1234 or visit www.relate.org.uk.

For more details of these organisations see the help list.

'Self-reverence, self-knowledge, self-control – these three alone lead life to sovereign power.'

Lord Alfred Tennyson.

Cognitive behavioural therapy (CBT)

When the government talks about training new therapists to help people cope with depression, they are referring to cognitive behavioural therapists.

Cognitive behavioural therapy aims to examine unwanted and negative thoughts and beliefs, and looks at ways of changing behaviour or reactions to these. It is based on the belief that thoughts and behaviour patterns build up over a long period of time with roots in the past.

It challenges thinking that has kept you stuck in the past or doing things that you don't understand. The therapist uses structured techniques to identify the thinking behind negative feelings and behaviour, and teaches skills to allow people to make changes and respond to events more positively.

Currently, CBT is not widely available on the NHS because of a lack of therapists, but the government is training several thousand therapists to provide patients with CBT instead of prescribing antidepressants. There is a CBT computer program that is supposed to be available to the public through the NHS, so it is worth asking your GP about it.

The British Association of Behavioural and Cognitive Psychotherapies, call 0161 797 4484 or visit www.babcp.com.

You could also take a look at *Cognitive Behavioural Therapy – The Essential Guide* by Dr Sara Pascoe, Need2Know, 2012.

Life coaching

There are times in life when you don't know what decision to make about your relationships, your job, where to live or how to help your children, but you may not feel that you are in need of counselling. If you feel that you need some guidance about what to do and how to sort out your life, life coaching could be for you.

Life coaching can be carried out either on the phone or in person, and it has recently become a popular career with some coaches specialising in business.

What is particularly good about life coaching is that it's like having a very good honest friend, who will point out the truth to you without being judgemental. The advantage is that, unlike a friend, a coach has no emotional involvement in your life and is not affected by outcomes. They tell you how it is and they are trained to help you make life more workable for you.

Life coaching is not available on the NHS and can only be accessed privately.

The Life Coaching Company gives free half hour sessions to anyone who calls them on 01628 488 990 or contacts them through their website www.lifecoaching-company.co.uk.

Neuro-Linguistic Programming (NLP)

NLP aims to change behaviour and thinking and in turn alter the way that you respond to things. Initially, you develop tools that help you to change your way of responding and eventually it becomes natural.

It is particularly helpful for anyone suffering from stress who would like to regain control, and it is widely used in helping people with addictions and phobias often in conjunction with hypnotherapy.

International NLP Trainers Association, call 023 925 88887 or visit www.inlpta.co.uk.

Hypnotherapy

Hypnotherapy is when you are taken into a state of deep relaxation but you are not actually asleep. In this state you are able to accept and respond to suggestions that can help you to change your ways. It is often used for people wanting to give up smoking, but can be more generally used to change your reaction to certain situations.

Before the session you talk to the hypnotherapist about the problem so that they know what you are trying to deal with. Therapists use a variety of methods to get you into a deep relaxed state, including talking quietly or asking you to look at a picture or something else in the room. When you are breathing deeply the hypnotherapist may ask you relevant questions and make suggestions, before slowly bringing you back to a normal conscious state.

General Hypnotherapy Register, visit www.general-hypnotherapy-register.com.

Taking control of your finances

You may be one of the many people who are struggling to make ends meet, and this does make life much more stressful. Even if you feel the rest of your life is in control, it is very hard to relax when you are worried about how to pay the bills. It is a fact of life that many people struggle with money and often have a family to feed and look after as well.

Do you have any of the following?

- Outstanding credit card bills that are incurring monthly interest.
- Outstanding loans.
- Permanent overdrafts at the bank.
- Debts of any other kind.

If your finances are in a mess it is a mistake to go to a debt adviser or consultant, as they usually end up costing you more and sometimes they are disreputable. You should never have to pay someone to help you out of debt.

The first port of call could be to the Citizens Advice Bureau, which is free of charge and completely neutral. They can provide free legal advice as well.

They can give you information about benefits and entitlements. For instance, if you earn less than £50,000 and you have children under 18, you are entitled to Family Tax Credit, and Working Tax Credit is available for people who earn much less than that.

One extremely helpful website is www.moneysavingexpert.com run by Martin Lewis who is now advising the government on student fees. He covers every angle of saving money and advises people what to do when they have been in debt, so you can find out about how to reduce household bills, get your son or daughter through university and much more. The site is worth referring to regularly to find out how to help yourself.

See *Working Mothers – The Essential Guide* (Need2Know) for more information on finances available for both parents.

Losing weight

When you start to uncover what is behind your stress, you may find there is something that is always bothering you. Being overweight may be sapping your energy and your confidence, and if you have been trying for a long time to slim down without success it can feel like a hopeless case.

There are so many new diets always appearing that it can be very confusing and often they are not very healthy or effective. In chapter 10 there is a section on eating healthily, which will help you lose weight. In addition to eating healthily, it is also important to take regular exercise to work off the calories that you are eating.

If you are having considerable trouble cutting down your weight, it may be worth joining one of the many clubs around the country:

Lighter Life, call 08002 988 988 or visit www.lighterlife.co.uk.

Weight Watchers, email uk.help@weightwatchers.co.uk or visit www.weightwatchers.co.uk.

Rosemary Conley, call 01509 620 222 or visit www.rosemaryconley.com.

Zest4Life Nutrition & Weight Loss, call 0845 603 9333 or visit www.zest4life.eu.

Are you SAD?

Seasonal affective disorder (SAD) is said to affect one million people in Britain alone and is particularly prevalent in countries that are further from the Equator – such as Scandinavia, Britain and Iceland.

There is a long list of symptoms and you may feel that some of them apply to you but that you're not too badly affected. People who have SAD seriously can be very unwell in the winter.

See if any of the following apply to you in winter only:

▪ Do you feel depressed when the days are short and dark?

▪ Do you find that in winter you have cravings for carbohydrates and sweet foods – pasta, rice, potatoes, sugary snacks, chocolate, biscuits or cakes?

▪ Do you feel tired all the time?

▪ Do you have mood swings?

▪ Do you feel less able to cope and very stressed?

▪ Are you prone to colds and flu?

- Are you lacking in energy?
- Does spring make you feel generally better?

If you have said yes to four or more of these and it happens every winter, you may be suffering from SAD.

One of the main reasons that people suffer from SAD is that less of the brain chemical serotonin is produced due to lack of daylight. Serotonin is responsible for hunger, thirst, sexual activity, sleep patterns, moods and body temperature and therefore, when there is not enough, all of these are disrupted.

There are several complementary therapies that can help, including nutrition, acupuncture, homeopathy and reflexology, but the most recognised treatment is light therapy. Lamps can be purchased to put at your desk at work or at home, or anywhere in the house – you only need half an hour a day under these full spectrum lights to make you feel better.

For more information contact SAD Association. Write to PO Box 989, Steyning, BN44 3HG, or visit www.sada.org.uk.

Summing Up

- There is plenty of help available in terms of talking therapies, and you can choose from counselling, cognitive behavioural therapy, life coaching or NLP.

- You may decide that you want a different approach and hypnotherapy helps you to change your reaction and behaviour patterns.

- You normally have to pay for many of these therapies, although some counselling and therapy is available on the NHS.

- There may be other issues that are making your stress worse, and these should be addressed.

- Finances can prove to be a considerable source of stress and if they are in a mess you need help in sorting them out.

- It may be that you have other niggling problems such as being overweight or suffering from Seasonal affective disorder.

- In today's more enlightened society there are always ways of helping yourself with all of these problems.

Chapter Nine

Lie Back and Relax

Some people choose to be busy all the time so that they don't have time to stop and think. Solitude and peace and quiet could be scary if there are things you don't want to face, but at some stage in your life the things you are trying to forget may well come back to haunt you. Better to sort out whatever it is now and really learn to relax, rather than making yourself ill.

If you can cope with being alone you feel stronger and less likely to be lonely if one day you are left alone. Feeling that you can cope alone means that you don't have to worry if 'what if' ever happens.

Is your lifestyle getting in the way of your wellbeing?

- Do you think that you haven't got enough time to relax?
- Do you believe that you can't fit exercise into your busy schedule?
- Do you find it easier to buy ready cooked meals or eat out than to cook a healthy meal?
- Do you feel as if you've never got enough time?

If you answer yes to three or more of these questions you are probably quite stressed and need to think about ways of learning to relax.

'Solitude and peace and quiet could be scary if there are things you don't want to face, but at some stage in your life the things you are trying to forget may well come back to haunt you. Better to sort out whatever it is now and really learn to relax, rather than making yourself ill.'

What relaxation means

Many people think of relaxing as something to do on an annual holiday, but to avoid stress it's important to learn to relax regularly. If your life is stressful and you find it hard to relax it might be helpful to learn how.

For many people relaxing means watching television and having a glass of wine, but while this may work when life is going quite well, it doesn't particularly arm you for tough times.

Making time

It's quite common when you are stressed to feel as if there's no time to do relaxation, and you can even become stressed trying to fit it in. If you don't manage it every day, try to plan some time in the week when you can dedicate 20 to 30 minutes to relaxing.

The more you relax, exercise and eat well, the less stressed you feel and you can cope more. When you're not well have you ever noticed how everything seems too difficult and you feel unable to cope with everyday chores? When you get better you can sort it all out in no time at all.

If you've been through a very difficult time you need to recuperate as if you've been ill. Be firm about looking after yourself, because no one else can do it for you.

Sleep well

Not getting enough sleep every night can make you stressed. New parents who are having interrupted nights with their baby find it less easy to cope because of their lack of sleep, and sometimes this goes on for months.

We tend to think that it's only young people who burn the candle at both ends, but many older people don't get enough sleep either. Millions of people don't sleep well, and even though some are disturbed by their partner's snoring, many lie awake worrying about things.

You will well know what it's like to look at the clock every hour while your mind is incredibly alert and keeps running over and over the same thing. It's a vicious circle – stress can interrupt your sleep, and not enough sleep can make you stressed.

Why you need a good night

The body repairs itself at night and recovers from all the anxieties of the day. If you never get a good night's sleep you are almost running on empty all the time. If you cannot sleep well at night on a regular basis you need to catch up at some time during the day.

Recent research in Greece showed that people who took siestas in the middle of their working day had lower levels of heart disease. Most British employers are unlikely to accept the siesta suggestion, but for anyone who isn't working or is self-employed, it can be fitted into your day. Many company CEOs and government leaders claim to have power naps or catnaps to keep them going.

Self-help tips for sleeping

- Develop a sleep routine – have a bath before bed or go to bed at the same time whenever possible.
- Try to wind down before bedtime with a book or a bath with two to three drops of lavender oil dispersed in it.
- Don't watch violent films or have the television on in the bedroom.
- Cut out caffeine in the evening – try decaffeinated drinks or herbal teas.
- Try not to drink alcohol after 7 or 8pm and see if it makes a difference.
- Put two or three drops of lavender oil on a tissue and keep it tucked under the pillow so you can breathe in the relaxing vapour.
- If your partner snores either wear ear plugs or sleep in another room.

'Recent research in Greece showed that people who took siestas in the middle of their working day had lower levels of heart disease. Most British employers are unlikely to accept the siesta suggestion, but for anyone who isn't working or is self-employed, it can be fitted into your day. Many company CEOs and government leaders claim to have power naps or catnaps to keep them going.'

Herbal and homeopathic remedies

- The Bach Flower Remedy White Chestnut helps to quell the racing mind – keep it by the bed and put a few drops in water or on your tongue.

- Provided you can take herbal medicine (check with a qualified herbalist or GP if you are on medication) you could take tablets or tincture containing valerian, passiflora, hops or avena sativa (oats), which are very calming and help you to sleep.

- Chamomile tea is also a good soother at night.

- All these products can be purchased from health food stores, some pharmacies and supermarkets or online.

The Sleep Council runs an Insomnia helpline, Monday to Friday 6pm to 8pm, call 020 8994 9874.

Relaxation techniques

To do relaxation properly you do need to set aside around 20 to 30 minutes – preferably every day. If it makes you gasp merely thinking about setting aside that much time each day, try to do it as often as you can.

You can relax lying down or sitting up and you can use a variety of different techniques. Some people are put off by the word 'meditation', believing it to have religious connotations or be too mystical for them. Meditation is simply a method of stilling the mind and trying not to be bombarded by thoughts, and there's nothing weird about it at all!

Benefits of meditation

It is generally agreed that meditation is done in silence. The idea is to free your mind of thoughts and therefore become more able to get in touch with your true self – your soul or your essence. This is, of course, much easier said than done and it takes a lot of practice to get to the stage where you don't have thoughts interrupting you.

Sometimes people say that they aren't any good at meditation because of their thoughts coming and going but this is normal for everyone. It takes time and practice to become able to clear the mind successfully, but the benefits are enormous.

- It is said that 20 minutes of meditation is equivalent to a night's sleep so you can imagine how refreshing it feels to do it every day.

- Meditation is believed to have several health benefits, including lowering blood pressure and heart rate, and boosting the immune system to fight disease.

- It is also claimed to reduce levels of cortisol and adrenaline in the bloodstream, which are abundant at times of stress.

- It helps you think more clearly and be more patient.

- It improves memory and concentration.

- It enables you to get in touch with your feelings, making you more decisive.

Above all, meditation makes you calmer and more able to tolerate difficult situations when they arise. It is a great tool to help you to cope with stress, and even if you are not doing it regularly, it is a good idea to put aside some time to completely relax when you're going through a bad time.

Types of meditation

There are many different types of meditation. Transcendental meditation involves the repetition of a mantra in your head – this is usually a Sanskrit word, such as 'so hum' and because it's a word that you don't understand it has no connotations. Try breathing in while silently saying 'so' and out with 'hum'.

You can adapt this kind of meditation by simply repeating 'one, two' and breathing in on 'one' and out on 'two'. When thoughts start to interrupt, you simply go back to the words and keep repeating them to yourself.

'Time is a created thing. To say "I don't have time" is like saying "I don't want to".'

Lao Tzu.

When you have had a good meditation session you are somewhere between sleep and being awake – you are not asleep but you feel that you have been off in a daydream. It's very relaxing and gets even better as you continue to practise. To find out more about transcendental meditation visit www.t-m.org. uk.

Physical relaxation

Lie down on the floor or a bed in a quiet room with your eyes closed. Have your legs slightly apart and your hands by your sides, just away from the body with palms upwards.

- Relax your head, face, ears, eyes and mouth. Scrunch up your face and let it go.

- Focus on your neck and let it release tension.

- Hunch your shoulders up to your ears and let them go.

- Continue down through the body, tighten your fists and let them go.

- When you get to your feet do the same and let them go.

- Stay in the relaxation position for 10 minutes or more if possible and then wake up your body slowly by wiggling your toes and moving upwards.

Try this palming exercise before you get up:

Rub your hands together to make them warm and hold them over your closed eyes. It is very relaxing.

Research on Transcendental Meditation (TM)

Two studies on transcendental meditation, which The Beatles learnt from the Maharishi in India in the 1960s, have found that levels of depression were reduced by 48%. Because depression increases the risk of heart attack, meditation has a knock-on effect of reducing attacks as well.

The Maharishi University of Management in Iowa collaborated with the Charles Drew University in Los Angeles and the University of Hawaii and findings were backed up by other academics. TM is practised by six million people worldwide and induces inner calm, greater concentration, peaceful approach to life, more energy, and greater motivation. Previous studies have shown that it can lower blood pressure, increase insulin resistance and benefit the nervous system.

The semi-supine position

Teachers of the Alexander Technique show clients how to relax in the semi-supine position for regular relaxation – lying on your back with knees raised and head supported.

- Put one or two paperbacks where you will place your head.

- Lie down on the floor or a hard couch – a bed is usually too soft.

- Bend your knees and have your feet flat on the floor.

- Put your head on your paperback books so it is slightly raised.

- Lie in this position and think about how to let go of tension in the muscles – you can work from the head down.

- Stay there for 10 to 20 minutes and allow your mind to let go too.

Breathing exercises

Most people shallow breathe which means there isn't enough oxygen getting into the lungs and subsequently into all the body's cells and organs. You may do this all the time, but when you are stressed you are far more likely to shallow breathe. This in turn makes you feel light-headed and lethargic and can lead to health problems.

Yoga breathing exercises help people to breathe deeply right through the chest and diaphragm, drawing air into the stomach.

Lie down or sit comfortably in a chair with both feet on the floor or cross-legged to carry out these breathing exercises.

Counting breath

* Breathe in to the count of four (or six if you can).
* Hold the breath for the count of four.
* Breathe out to the count of four.

Repeat this cycle five times and see how relaxed you feel. If you feel at all light-headed cut down the amount of time you hold the breath for.

Alternate nostril breathing

* Close your right nostril with your right thumb and rest the next two fingers on your forehead while you breathe in through the left nostril.
* Then put your ring finger on the left nostril and breathe out through the right nostril, then breathe in again through the right nostril.

Continue with the same pattern for up to 10 cycles.

Emergency breathing

When you are in a highly stressful situation, sit down and close your eyes. Breathe as slowly and deeply as you can to calm yourself down.

Relaxation tapes and music

Some people find that they can relax best with some background music or guided meditation. You can buy relaxation tapes that guide you into a peaceful place or choose any soothing music or your own favourite classical or contemporary choice.

Visualisation

Creative visualisation is often used with cancer patients to help them to relax. Lying in bed or sitting in a comfortable position, you close your eyes and imagine a beautiful place – somewhere you may have been to before, in the mountains, by the sea or in a field. Start to see yourself lying there in the warm sunshine, with the birds singing in the background and nature all around you. It's a very relaxing and soothing thing to do and can help you to chill out completely.

There is another method of using visualisation which athletes sometimes do to help them win. They imagine what it will be like to win and how they will feel and see themselves picking up the prize. To adapt this to stressful situations, you could imagine several years hence when the problem you are currently encountering is over and you have achieved what you want to.

If you are ill, you can imagine your body being healthy again and visualise how it will feel emotionally and physically. Do this every day.

Exercise is relaxing

It may seem like a contradiction in terms to say that exercise is relaxing, but it is mentally relaxing. Just going for a brisk walk can calm you down and make you feel better. Making sure that you exercise four or five times a week is likely to reduce your stress levels.

Summing Up

- Relaxation means more than just sitting in front of the television. It needs some time and dedication, but it is incredibly worthwhile for helping you to prevent and ease stress.

- There are a variety of different relaxation techniques that you can choose from or you may prefer to try breathing exercises.

- Sleeping well is very important for both mental and physical health and there is plenty you can do to try to ensure you get a good night.

- Whichever way you achieve it, there is no doubt that relaxation is one of the most effective ways of combating stress.

Chapter Ten

Healthy Living

Exercise – the great de-stressor

All exercise is good for your health and wellbeing. Whether you like cycling, playing tennis, rugby, football, running, working out at the gym, trampolining, swimming, walking or dancing, it's all good for you physically and mentally.

Exercise releases endorphins, which are the chemicals in the brain that make you feel good and are known as 'happy hormones'.

When you feel lethargic, depressed and under stress it's easy to feel as if you don't want to exercise, but it can make you feel much better and take you out of yourself. If you regularly exercise, keep it up, but if you are starting for the first time try to choose something that you will enjoy. You're not going to want to do it if you don't enjoy it.

'People find life entirely too time-consuming.'
Stanislaw J. Lee.

It's your choice

Many people like going to the gym and having their own personalised workout. You might prefer to get out in the open and enjoy nature while you're exercising, so walking or running might suit you well. If you like dogs there's no greater incentive to exercise than having one to walk every day.

It often takes a change of mindset to get more exercise into your day without altering your schedule, for example, you could walk to work, the station or bus stop, or take the stairs instead of the lift.

Doing exercise doesn't mean that you have to be competitive or take up team sports that you don't enjoy. There are a whole range of choices that are good for you, including:

- Tennis.
- Walking.
- Dancing.
- Skipping.
- Trampolining (on a small home bouncer).
- Cycling.
- Gym exercises.
- Swimming.

Apart from helping you to relax and making you fit, exercise has many health benefits including prevention of arthritis, heart disease, osteoporosis and cancer. It helps you to keep weight off and prevent obesity, which is the cause of many illnesses.

Exercise for the mind

There are some forms of exercise that benefit you in the same way as the others, but have an added dimension. Yoga, t'ai chi and chi kung (qi gong) have the added advantage that they help to focus your mind and keep you calm.

Yoga

Yoga breathing exercises have been outlined in chapter 9, but yoga is an all-encompassing practice which has positive effects on the mind, body and spirit.

In a yoga class you learn to do postures which you do at your own pace – there is no pressure to be competitive or the best in the class. These are designed to fully exercise the body, stretching the muscles and bringing health benefits to all the organs.

There is also plenty of relaxation and breathing designed to help you stay calm. Yoga is something you need to do over a period of time to gain mental and physical benefits, and you can do it at home as often as you like.

To find a yoga teacher visit the British Wheel of Yoga at www.bwy.org.uk or call 01529 306851.

You could also take a look at *Yoga - The Essential Guide* by Sarah Dawson, Need2Know, 2011.

T'ai chi and chi kung

Only those people who do t'ai chi or chi kung (also known as qi gong) can understand how incredibly relaxing it is.

Chi kung is less well known than t'ai chi, but many people practise both, as they are both particularly good for the mind and the body. Chi kung consists of a variety of different exercises or movements that are gentle and repetitive. They have a positive effect on the mind and body and are based on the principle that they help to balance the energy – or chi – in your body.

They have become popular among older people, and in some areas chi kung and t'ai chi have been offered on the NHS instead of medication.

Exercises can be carried out with the eyes closed and they help to generate 'chi' or energy which can often be felt as tingling in the hands. Consequently, chi kung is very relaxing and it is believed to stimulate the immune system and modulate levels of stress.

T'ai chi is different from chi kung in that it consists of a form – a set number of exercises in a particular sequence that have to be learnt. One of the reasons why t'ai chi is considered to be very good for stress is that you have to concentrate on the movements and remember them. This is good for the memory but it also enables the mind to shut off other thoughts and that is why it is sometimes called 'moving meditation'.

There are plenty of classes around the country and they are usually very inexpensive, but are becoming more popular.

To find t'ai chi classes visit www.taichifinder.co.uk.

Eat to combat stress

Eating a healthy diet gives you the strength to cope with stress when it arises. As well as eating the right foods, it is also a question of eliminating food and drink that could be making you feel unwell.

Healthy eating

'Eating a healthy diet gives you the strength to cope with stress when it arises. As well as eating the right foods, it is also a question of eliminating food and drink that could be making you feel unwell.'

Nutritional deficiency affects the brain as well as the rest of body, disrupting your feelings and behaviour and making you less able to deal with stress. It is a common belief that your food should provide you with the amount of vitamins and minerals that you need, but this is not always the case.

Crops that have been sprayed with pesticides and grown in soil that is over-farmed and depleted of nutrients do not provide the required levels of minerals or vitamins. In this stressful world in which we all live, there are numerous reasons why your immune system is run down, including environmental pollution, chemicals in food, cosmetics, household cleansing products, over-processed food, smoking, alcohol and other stimulants.

There are several benefits to eating organic food:

- It is not tainted by manmade chemicals such as pesticides.

- Animals are reared in a free-range environment, fed appropriate food and not given drugs routinely.

- It contains more nutrients (vitamins and minerals) because crops are rotated and the soil is not over-farmed.

What are healthy foods?

People rightly get confused and annoyed by all the conflicting news that they hear about food – one minute something is good for you and the next it isn't. However, there are some food facts that don't change.

- Fruit and vegetables provide vitamins and minerals – even though they are better if they are organically produced.

- Oily fish is high in essential fats, which are required for healthy brain function, a healthy heart and mobile joints.

- Wholegrains such as wholemeal bread, oats, brown rice and pasta have not had the goodness taken out (unlike white bread, pasta and rice).

- Pulses such as beans, split peas and lentils are high in nutrients.

- Water is the best drink you can have. It doesn't have to be mineral water, filtered tap water is a good option.

What's your poison?

How often do you consume the following?

- Salt.

- Coffee.

- Alcohol.

- Saturated fats – butter, full cream milk, red meat.

- Processed foods (those made in a factory).

- Hydrogenated fats (in pies, some spreads and other processed food).

- Fizzy drinks.

If you have three or more of these every day of the week you may be building up health problems for the future.

Why they are not good for you

- Too much salt – can raise blood pressure.

- Coffee – has many effects but caffeine can raise blood pressure, make you more uptight and keep you awake.

- Alcohol – stimulates you in the short term, but depresses you in the long term and can lead to addiction.

- Saturated fats – builds up unhealthy cholesterol in the arteries, leading to heart disease and strokes.

- Processed foods – these contain salt, sugar and many unwanted E numbers that could be making you hyper.
- Hydrogenated fats – they stop your body absorbing healthy nutrients.
- Fizzy drinks – contain a variety of manmade chemicals such as flavourings, colourings and sweeteners, sugar and caffeine.

Drinking – from alcohol to coffee

Sharing a bottle of wine every evening is quite normal for many people but recent research has shown that people are using alcohol to cope with their stress. Mothers of young children or people who are working hard often feel that they deserve a few glasses of wine after a hard day to help them unwind.

'Drinking is a very acceptable part of our culture, but exceeding government guidelines on a regular basis can cause depression and physical illness. Hospital consultants are now seeing far more young people in their 20s and 30s with cirrhosis of the liver, a disease that used to afflict the over 50s only.

If drinking is used as a stress-release tool and no other measures are taken, it can get out of hand. If you feel that it is too difficult to stop drinking alcohol you can get help from Alcoholics Anonymous (see opposite).

Learning to manage stress in the long run is a better method of dealing with it than blotting it out through drink or drugs. This, of course, is much easier said than done and if someone is stressed, and drinking is their solution, they are unlikely to be able to just stop immediately.

It is often tempting to take the easy route for short-term enjoyment – drinking to cope with stress, watching television rather than making the effort to exercise or eating what you like. In the long term this can be far more difficult to deal with because you can become unhealthy and overweight.

Adopting a long-term strategy takes courage and is difficult when you are feeling overwhelmed with problems. But if your health is not to suffer, it is probably time to talk to someone about your stress.

You could approach:

- Your GP who may be able to recommend counselling.

- An independent counsellor.

- A spiritual or religious leader.

- Support groups such as Alcoholics Anonymous, or Cruse if you have been bereaved.

For more detailed information, see *Alcoholism – The Family Guide* (Need2Know).

Getting help

Drinkline, for confidential help if you are concerned about drinking too much call 0800 917 8282.

Talk to Frank, for help and support if you are concerned about someone who is taking drugs, call 0800 77 66 00 or visit www.talktofrank.com.

Alcoholics Anonymous (AA) – every Yellow Pages has a local listing. Meetings involve structured group therapy with people discussing their problems in a caring environment. Call the national helpline 0845 769 7555 or visit www.alcoholics-anonymous.org.uk.

Once you accept that you (or the person you are concerned about) have a problem, it is the first step towards recovery. You can then go about getting help.

Alcohol and stress – a heady mix

It's a telling fact that a recent British survey of adults found that the main reasons for having a drink in the evening were connected to stress.

Nearly three quarters (72%) of women said they pour themselves a glass of wine to relax, as opposed to 57% of men. The survey of 825 ABC1 working adults found that:

- 65% drank after a stressful day.

- 53% had a drink as a result of a bad day at work.

- Only 15% had a drink because of a great day.

Some 60% of the women claimed that they have two or more large glasses of wine a night (double the recommended daily unit guidelines), and 64% of men said that they drink two pints of beer on an average day.

While it is a popular way of unwinding, drinking alcohol to de-stress is more likely to make the situation worse. According to experts it can have the opposite effect by:

- Affecting sleep patterns.

- Making you wake up feeling more stressed because of a poor night.

- Making you feel more irritable and tired.

Government recommended drinking units:

- 14 units a week for women.

- 21 units a week for men.

- A pint of beer (4%) = two units.

- 330ml bottle of beer (5%) = two units.

- 175ml glass of wine (12%) = two units.

- 25ml single shot of spirits (40%) = one unit.

More information can be found from MyDrinkaware (www.mydrinkaware.co.uk)

How alcohol affects daily life

The survey also illustrates the impact that alcohol has on the domestic evening routine. When respondents were asked what they do to unwind at home, pouring a glass of wine was cited as the second most popular option (61%) after chilling out in front of the TV. Putting their feet up with a drink to relax after a stressful day ranks higher than wanting to spend time with their children (28%), or talk with one another (26%).

Donna Dawson, a psychologist specialising in Personality and Behaviour, says:

'When it comes to drinking alcohol, the way the human brain works means we are naturally disposed to find a reason to indulge, particularly if we've had a tough day. An example of this is having a drink or two at home after work as a way to unwind from stress – in this scenario, the brain has decided that stress is bad for us, and that alcohol, because it apparently relieves stress, is good.

'So, at the end of the day, we may know that the second or third glass of alcohol is not really needed or even desired, but the brain has already rationalised that if one glass felt good, then more will feel even better. What we need to do is recognise this is faulty brain-reasoning at work and take more conscious control of why, when and how much we drink, as well as the health harms that alcohol can cause.'

In July 2011, Vision Critical surveyed a sample of 825 ABC1 working adults. 461 were 30-46 working adults, the target audience for 'What's Your Excuse'.

The effects of alcohol on stressed-out people

A study which appeared in the October 2011 edition of Alcoholism: Clinical & Experimental Research, looked at the effects of alcohol on stressed people.

According to the study's corresponding author, Emma Childs of The University of Chicago, 'Stress could increase drinking by altering alcohol's effects. For example, if stress reduces the intoxicating effects of alcohol, individuals may drink more alcohol to produce the same effect.'

According to Childs, there are very different physiological and emotional consequences along a timeline after the onset of stress. A racing heart, raised blood pressure, production of the hormone cortisol, feelings of tension, and depression reduce at different rates from each other. With alcohol, the impact varies according to when it was drunk.

The study looked at 25 healthy men who, in two sessions, performed a stressful public speaking task – and a non-stressful control task. It's quite common for public speaking to bring on physiological signs of stress. After each task, the participants were administered an infusion containing the same amount of alcohol you'd find in two drinks – and a placebo.

One group of participants received the infusion within one minute of task completion, followed by a placebo 30 minutes later. The other group received the placebo first, then the alcohol and the responses were measured at different times.

Emma Childs said, 'Alcohol can change the way that the body deals with stress: it can decrease the hormone cortisol which the body releases to respond to stress, and it can prolong the feelings of tension produced by the stress. Stress can also change how alcohol makes a person feel: it can reduce the pleasant effects of alcohol or increase craving for more alcohol.'

The study revealed that alcohol decreased the hormonal response to stress and extended the negative subjective experience of the stressful event.

'Stress responses are beneficial in that they help us to react to adverse events. By altering the way that our bodies deal with stress, we may be increasing the risks of developing stress-related diseases, not the least of which is alcohol addiction,' according to Emma Childs.

Short-term boosts: coffee, cigarettes and chocolate

A lot of us feel that we can only keep going if we have endless cups of coffee to wake up our brains, or that cigarettes keep us calm, and chocolate provides the pleasure we feel we are lacking when times get difficult. What's more, they are not illegal and you're not doing anyone else any harm, so what's the problem?

The problems with caffeine and sugar are that they actually make us worse in the long term. Caffeine has an effect on blood sugar levels so that you have highs and lows. Most people are familiar with slumping mid-afternoon and needing a snack to keep them going. This is when blood sugar levels have dipped and the more caffeine you drink, the more they go haywire.

Supplementing your diet

When the adrenal glands produce adrenaline, stores of glucose are released into the blood and insulin has to be produced by the pancreas to remove excess glucose from the blood. Blood sugar levels go awry and the body becomes out of balance trying to stabilise them. This is often when you reach for sugary snacks or caffeine to keep going, but consequently you feel as if you have no energy.

Nutritionists recommend you need food supplements all the time and usually recommend a multivitamin/mineral be taken every day. It is particularly important to take extra vitamins and minerals when you are stressed.

Vitamins and minerals

The following are vital at times of stress:

Vitamin B – most B vitamins turn glucose into energy and are required for healthy brain function. B6 is often taken by women as an antidepressant and for PMS or menopausal symptoms. There are B vitamins in many vegetables, seeds, nuts, fish, turkey and chicken.

Vitamin C – fights illness and keeps the immune system healthy but is instrumental in making anti-stress hormones and turning food into energy. Extra should be taken at times of stress and illness – if you take too much the body excretes it. Most fruit is high in vitamin C, as are many vegetables.

Folic acid – is essential for nerve and brain function and for the development of the unborn child. It is found in broccoli, peanuts, spinach, wheatgerm, asparagus, avocado and walnuts.

Calcium – is needed for healthy nerves, bones and teeth and helps you to sleep. A deficiency in calcium can account for insomnia or nervousness as well as physical problems. It is available in dairy products, broccoli, artichokes, almonds, parsley and cabbage.

Iron – provides energy by transporting oxygen to cells and if deficient you can become anaemic, tired and listless. Iron is found in liver, Brazil nuts, walnuts, parsley, pumpkin seeds and sesame seeds.

Zinc – is essential for a healthy nervous system, for energy and fighting stress. It is found in oysters, oats, shrimps, haddock, eggs, wholewheat, rye, peanuts and almonds.

Chromium – helps to stabilise blood sugar levels and is in wholemeal bread, eggs, rye, oysters, potatoes, chicken, parsnips, potatoes and apples.

Vitamins A, E, beta-carotene, selenium, copper, manganese, potassium, and magnesium are also needed for helping the body to cope with stress. A good multivitamin/mineral provides all of the vitamins and minerals mentioned.

The role of probiotics

Probiotics encourage a healthy gut by introducing friendly bacteria which are often destroyed when you are under stress. When the healthy bacteria are destroyed they are usually replaced by hostile bacteria which cause stomach problems. That is why you are prone to stomach problems, ulcers and irritable bowel when you are going through difficult times.

As the gut is responsible for the health of the immune system, it follows that keeping it in good shape is more likely to keep you feeling well. You are more able to fight stress if your body is in good condition. Probiotics are added to many foods and are in live yoghurt, but to get the amount you need it is better to take capsules.

Omega-3s

Omega-3s from oily fish such as mackerel, herring, tuna, sardines and salmon, are essential fats that are required by the brain for healthy function.

When you are under stress it is very helpful to provide the brain with the essential nutrients it needs. Omega-3s can improve sleep, relieve depression and boost the functioning of the nervous system. They are sometimes given to children with learning difficulties or people with Alzheimer's and have been shown to produce good results.

Summing Up

- Eating healthy food and doing regular exercise builds up your strength and ability to fight illness.

- Resorting to stimulants, such as coffee, cigarettes, drugs and booze can only bring short-term relief. Eventually they affect your health adversely and make your life even more difficult than it was in the first place.

- To be in a healthy state to cope with stress you need plenty of nutrients (vitamins and minerals and other supplements) from your food, so eating a good diet full of fruit and vegetables is vital.

- To ensure that you get enough vitamins and minerals you might need to take food supplements when you are going through a difficult time.

Chapter Eleven

Complementary Medicine

The majority of the public has now tried complementary medicine in some form or another, whether it's taking a herbal remedy or going to an acupuncturist. The benefit of complementary therapies and remedies is that they enable you to take control of your own wellbeing.

Obviously you shouldn't overlook serious illness, but when you are feeling stressed there are things you can do to help yourself.

Little helpers

In these days of alternative remedies, there are many lotions and potions available to help you have a relaxing bath or breathe in soothing vapours.

Lavender oil

Lavender has soothing properties, and for a relaxing bath put two or three drops in the water. Disperse the oil with your hand, lie back in the warm bath and relax. You can also choose geranium or sandalwood to relax, or if you need to be reinvigorated put in a few drops of rosemary oil.

Flower remedies

There are now several ranges of flower essences and remedies: Bach Flower Remedies, Bush Flower Essences and Jan de Vries Essences cater for a variety of emotions. Different plants are believed to address specific states of mind and may ease negative emotions, helping you at times of stress.

Rescue Remedy and Emergency Essence are combinations of remedies that are helpful during traumatic events or when you are feeling stressed. They can be purchased from chemists, health food stores, online and from some supermarkets.

If you keep a bottle with you all the time, you can put some drops on the tongue if you have an accident or a frightening incident occurs

Put a few drops of the most appropriate remedies in water and sip all day. You can find flower remedies to help with confidence, bereavement, guilt and many other feelings. It is often a helpful way to find out what exactly you are feeling.

> 'The doctor of the future will give no medicine but will interest his patients in the care of the human frame, in diet, and in the cause and prevention of disease.'
>
> Thomas Edison.

Herbal medicine

Consult a registered medical herbalist or a doctor before taking remedies if you are on medication or have a medical condition.

- Valerian is a great calming remedy in times of stress – you can take tincture in water several times a day or buy tablets.
- Passiflora from the passion flower is also calming and soothing and can be taken the same way.
- Avena sativa is the tincture of oats which are known to have calming properties.

Some of the herbal calming tablets you find in health food stores combine several of these remedies with other herbs. They are not addictive and make a good alternative to antidepressants, which have recently had a bad press due to their side effects and ineffectiveness.

Complementary therapies

People who are keen to prevent ill health find that complementary therapies help to keep them aware of their state of health and in touch with both mind and body. Many therapies are so relaxing that they ease stress as well as helping with other health issues.

Followers of complementary medicine prefer a holistic approach to health, acknowledging that the mind, body and spirit are all connected, and that emotional health dictates physical health. Some conventional doctors are averse to complementary or natural medicine because it is not always scientifically proven.

The public are voting with their feet and are using more and more natural remedies and therapies. Some people are fed up with being offered drugs as the only solution to their problems, or they find that therapies work better for them than conventional medicine.

There are only a few complementary therapies available on the NHS, including chiropractic and osteopathy which can be referred by your GP. Acupuncture, homeopathy and herbal medicine are available in some areas of the health service and there are currently five NHS homeopathic hospitals in the UK.

For most other therapies it is necessary to pay, except in situations where you have cancer or are caring for someone who has it. There are many voluntary organisations providing free therapies for cancer patients and their carers, and this may be the case in your area for other illnesses too.

What happens in a session?

A visit to a complementary therapist usually lasts for 40 minutes to an hour and can be even longer. Many of them want to know about your medical and personal history as this enables them to understand what the root of the problem is.

Sometimes you can discover that things that happened when you were a child have affected your health ever since. Or it may be more recent events that are affecting you, for example if you are being bullied at work, you might have physical symptoms but have not connected them to your job situation.

Receiving such extended one-to-one attention compares well with the five or 10 minutes GPs can offer you. It helps you to feel that you are being listened to, which makes you feel better and more receptive.

The following therapies can help with stress:

Massage comes in all shapes and sizes these days. The many different types include:

- Hot stone massage – heated large stones are placed on your back and used to massage it, warming and soothing muscles.

- Indian head massage which includes neck and shoulders too. You don't need to take your clothes off for this, and it's very relaxing.

- Swedish massage is usually very deep getting right into muscles and kneading them so that you feel invigorated afterwards. Can be helpful for aches and pains.

Reflexology involves the use of hands to massage or knead the foot in specific areas which relate to parts of the body. It's a thoroughly relaxing therapy as you lie back and may even fall asleep. It is particularly known to have a positive effect on the endocrine system, which is responsible for hormones and is adversely affected by stress. Association of Reflexologists, call 01823 351010 or visit www.aor.org.uk.

Aromatherapy involves full body, head, neck or back massage with essential oils. Essential oils are made from plants and are said to have therapeutic properties for both physical and emotional wellbeing. Lavender, geranium, and chamomile are particularly good for relaxing the mind and body. A massage is a pleasant experience which can make you feel nurtured and pampered. If you cannot afford to pay for an aromatherapy massage you can buy the essential oils and persuade your partner to do it instead. The International Federation of Professional Aromatherapists, call 01455 637987 or visit www.ifparoma.org.

Acupuncture involves the placing of fine needles on the acupressure points along the body's meridians. Acupuncture clears energy blocks in the meridians allowing free flow of energy, or a rush of blood to the area, with the result that you feel better, both mentally and physically. British Acupuncture Council, call 020 8735 0400 or visit www.acupuncture.org.uk.

The Alexander Technique enables you to be aware of your posture and where you are causing tension in the body. Everyone tenses up in certain places when they are stressed and this can lead to muscle tightness and pain. By learning to be aware of when and where you are doing this you can release tension, which is both relaxing and beneficial to your health. The Society for Teachers of the Alexander Technique, call 0207 482 5135 or visit www.stat.org. uk.

Homeopathy is a gentle system of medicine which involves diluted extracts from plants and minerals available in a small sugar pill. They are completely safe for any age group, even if you are on medication. The homeopath spends a long time taking details of a person's characteristics, likes and dislikes, as well as their physical symptoms and treats the person as a whole. It can be very effective for stress. The British Homeopathic Association, call 01582 408675 or visit www.trusthomeopathy.org.

Herbal Medicine involves the use of natural plant tinctures (or tablets) to bring about change in the body. Herbal tinctures and tablets such as valerian and passiflora are renowned for their calming properties, as is avena sativa, which is made from oats. St John's wort is good for relieving depression, but if you are taking medication you must check with either your doctor or your medical herbalist that the herbs do not contraindicate the medicine. National Institute of Medical Herbalists, call 01392 426022 or visit www.nimh.org.uk.

Naturopathy looks at you as a whole and is particularly concerned with what is happening to you emotionally. One of its main premises is to discover if you are being bullied by anyone in your life – this is not always obvious to the person involved. Naturopaths may suggest changes in diet and natural remedies such as homeopathy, herbal remedies or flower essences to help the person to recover. Register of Naturopaths, British Naturopathic Association, call 01485 840072 or visit www.naturopathy.org.uk.

Reiki is a form of healing which draws negative energy away from the body and helps you to relax. When you go for a treatment you lie on a couch while the healer moves around you, usually holding their hands just above you. It's very relaxing and you are quite likely to fall asleep or doze. There are many volunteer healing groups that ask for small donations of around £5, so reiki healing can be a very sensible option if you cannot afford much. The Reiki Association, email enquiries@reikiassociation.org.uk or visit www. reikiassociation.org.uk.

Emotional Freedom Technique (EFT) has become very popular recently, and although there are therapists who offer it, it is easy to learn and practise self-help. EFT involves identifying the problem and repeating relevant words

'Stress covers the many trials and tribulations of modern life that have a negative impact on body, mind and soul,'

Jan de Vries, naturopath and author of *Emotional Healing*.

while tapping on specific acupressure points. The aim is to release long-held negative emotions. Emotional Freedom Technique Academy, www.eft-academy.co.uk.

Summing Up

- Complementary therapies have become increasingly popular in the last 20 years, yet few are available on the NHS.

- Chiropractic and osteopathy are registered for referral by doctors, and acupuncture, homeopathy and herbal medicine can be accessed in some areas. They are particularly suitable for stress because therapists give you one-to-one attention in a relaxed environment and can help to ease both emotional and physical pain.

- There are a number of natural remedies you can buy over the counter to keep yourself calm as well.

Help List

Support for individuals

Alcoholics Anonymous

PO Box 1, 10 Toft Green, York, YO1 7NJ
National helpline: 0845 769 7555 (24 hours)
www.alcoholics-anonymous.org.uk
Provides help and therapy for those affected by alcohol and their relatives.

Alcohol Concern

Suite B5, West Wing, New City Cloisters, 196 Old Street, London EC1V 9FR
Tel: 020 7264 0510 (Monday to Friday, 1pm-5pm)
www.alcoholconcern.org.uk
Information and advice for those worried about their drinking habits or those of
someone else.

Association for Coaching

www.associationforcoaching.com
This organisation has an online register of accredited coaches.

British Association of Anger Management

Tel: 0345 1300 286 (Monday to Friday, 9am-5pm)
info@angermanage.co.uk
www.angermanage.co.uk
Professional body of consultants, counsellors and trainers. Provides individual
support, workshops, seminars and training packages.

British Association of Behavioural and Cognitive Psychotherapies

Victoria Buildings, 9-13 Silver Street, Bury, BL9 0EU
Tel: 0161 797 4484

babcp@babcp.com
www.babcp.com
Provides a list of accredited cognitive behavioural and rational-emotive therapists. These therapies teach you to change behaviour in response to certain triggers.

British Association for Counselling and Psychotherapy (BACP)

BACP House, 15 St John's Business Park, Lutterworth, LE17 4HB
Tel: 0870 443 5252
www.bacp.co.uk
Main body for accreditation of counsellors and can provide details of local therapists.

Counselling Directory

www.counselling-directory.org.uk
Directory of counsellors and psychotherapists who can help you to deal with stress.

Cruse Bereavement Care

Tel: 0844 477 9400 (Day by Day helpline)
Tel: 0808 808 1677 (free calls for young persons)
helpline@cruse.org.uk
Email for young people: info@rd4u.org.uk
www.cruse.org.uk

General Hypnotherapy Register

PO Box 204, Lymington, SO41 6WP
www.general-hypnotherapy-register.com
Provides a register of hypnotherapists.

One Plus One

www.oneplusone.org.uk
OnePlusOne is a UK-based charity that analyses relationship research, and uses the evidence to create relationship-building resources for parents, couples and people working with families.

The Institute of Family Therapy (IFT)

24-32 Stephenson Way, London, NW1 2HX
Tel: 0207 391 9150
www.instituteoffamilytherapy.org.uk
Provides free counselling to families, and is located near to Euston Station,
London. People can come from any area to see the trained counsellors.

The Life Coaching Company

Tel: 01628 488 990
www.lifecoaching-company.co.uk
This company gives free half hour sessions to anyone who calls them or
contacts them through their website.

Relate

Tel: 0300 100 1234
www.relate.org.uk
Provides relationship counselling to married or cohabiting couples, individuals
and teenagers. Teenagers whose parents are separating can speak in
confidence to a counsellor free of charge.

SAD Association

PO Box 989, Steyning, BN44 3HG
www.sada.org.uk
The SAD Association is a voluntary organisation which informs the public
and health professions about SAD and supports and advises sufferers of the
illness.

Working Families

www.workingfamilies.org.uk

Simply Health

www.simplyhealth.co.uk

Be Mindful Online

www.bemindfulonline.com

Cancer support

Carers UK

20 Great Dover Street, London SE1 4LX
Tel: 020 7378 4999
www.carersuk.org
Provides information and support to relatives, friends and professional carers.
Has branches throughout the UK and can put you in contact with support
groups. Visit the website for contact details for Scotland and Wales.

Teenage Cancer Trust

3rd Floor, 93 Newman Street, London, W1T 3EZ
Tel: 020 7612 0370
tct@teenagecancertrust.org
www.teenagecancertrust.org
For teenagers who have cancer, and their families. It offers a local support
network and there is an online forum on the website where teens can
communicate with others in the same situation as themselves.

Workplace stress organisations

Advisory, Conciliation and Arbitration Service (ACAS)

Tel: 08457 474747 (Monday to Friday, 8am-8pm)
www.acas.org.uk
ACAS provides free eLearning packages for individuals on subjects including
bullying and harassment, age discrimination, managing absence and working
parents. Visit the website for details of all regional offices.

Business Balls

www.businessballs.com
This is a helpful website with lots of tips and information about handling stress at work.

Centre for Stress Management

Broadway House, 3 High Street, Bromley, BR1 1LF
Tel: 020 8228 1185
www.managingstress.com
This is an international training centre and stress consultancy. It undertakes stress management and prevention programmes, stress audits and research, stress counselling, coaching and training.

Chartered Institute of Personnel and Development (CIPD)

151 The Broadway, London, SW19 1JQ
Tel: 020 8612 6200
www.cipd.co.uk
This is an organisation for HR personnel, provides information and books on all subjects concerning personnel in the workplace.

Employment Tribunals

Tel: 0845 795 9775 (Monday to Friday, 9am-5pm)
www.employmenttribunals.gov.uk
The Employment Tribunals are judicial bodies who determine disputes between employers and employees over employment rights. The website provides information about the tribunal's procedures and gives guidance on how you make or respond to a claim.

Health and Safety Executive (HSE)

Tel: 0845 345 0055
www.hse.gov.uk
This government-run organisation is responsible for health and safety matters in industry and commerce, including stress. Provides advice and publications.

The International Stress Management Association UK (ISMA)

PO Box 108, Caldicot, Monmouthshire NP26 9AP
Tel: 0845 680 7083
www.isma.org.uk
A registered charity with multi-disciplinary professional membership. Promotes sound knowledge and best practice in the prevention, reduction and management of personal and work-related stress. It also sets professional standards for the benefit of individuals or organisations using the services of members.

The Samaritans

The Upper Mill, Kingston Road, Ewell, Surrey, KT17 2AF
UK Tel: 08457 909090 (emergency line for anyone needing help)
Republic of Ireland: 1850 60 90 90
www.samaritans.org
The Samaritans runs WorkLife training courses on tackling stress in the workplace for both managers and teams.

The Stress Management Society

Tel: 0808 231 6211
info@stress.org.uk
www.stress.org.uk
Provides workplace stress management courses and workshops to companies.

UK National Work-Stress Network

www.workstress.net
Provides information on stress and advice to companies about stress among employees. Has a regular newsletter.

Work Life Balance Centre

Tel: 01530 273056
www.worklifebalancecentre.org
This organisation provides information and research about stress at work.

Work Smart (from Trades Union Council)

www.worksmart.org.uk

Provides information for employees about your rights, how to deal with problems at work, where to get help and more.

Bibliography

Managing the causes of work-related stress – A step-by-step approach using the Management Standards – (HSG218 ISBN 9780717662739) is now available from Health and Safety Executive Books priced £10.95, www.hse.gov.uk.

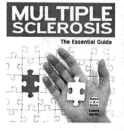